TRANSFORMATIONAL THOUGHT II:
MORE RADICAL IDEAS TO REMAKE
THE BUILT ENVIRONMENT

An Ecotone Publishing Book/2016

Copyright ©2016 by Jason F. McLennan

**Ecotone Publishing – an Imprint of
International Living Future Institute**

All rights reserved. No part of this publication may be reproduced, distributed or transmitted in any form or by any means, including photocopying, recording, or other electronic or mechanical methods, without the prior written permission of the publisher, except in the case of brief quotations embodied in critical reviews and certain other noncommercial uses permitted by copyright law. For permission requests, write to the publisher, addressed "Attention Permissions Coordinator," at the address below.

For more information write:

Ecotone Publishing
721 NW Ninth Avenue, Suite 195
Portland, OR 97209

Author: Jason F. McLennan with contributions by Bill Reed

Book Design: softfirm

Cover Photograph: Johan Bergmark

Edited by: Joanna Gangi and Fred McLennan

Library of Congress Control Number: 2016931945

Library of Congress Cataloging-in Publication Data

ISBN: 978-0-9972368-0-4

1. Architecture   2. Environment   3. Philosophy

First Edition

Printed in Canada on FSC-certified paper, processed Chlorine-Free, using vegetable-based ink.

This book is dedicated to my wonderful children who make every day special to me.

Rowan Isla McLennan

Aidan Finlay McLennan

Declan Gabriel McLennan

Julian Henry Willett

TRANSFORMATIONAL THOUGHT II:
MORE RADICAL IDEAS TO REMAKE THE BUILT ENVIRONMENT

Essays by Jason F. McLennan

8	**FOREWORD** by Bill Reed
12	**SO TOO CAN WE** A Poem of Regeneration
14	**A SUSTAINED AWAKENING OF THE HUMAN HEART: LOVE AND GREEN BUILDING** A Small Musing on a Big Subject
22	**A LIVING COMMUNITY ON EARTH** The Swelling Horde, Carrying Capacity and a Constrained World
38	**LIVING COMMUNITIES OF THE FUTURE**
48	**PASSING THROUGH THE BOTTLENECK** Humanity's Final Gamble
66	**THE BOUNDARY OF DISCONNECT** Life, Resilience & a Question of Scale
78	**REGENERATING THE WHOLE** From Living Buildings to Building Life *with Bill Reed*
94	**FALLING IN LOVE WITH LIFE** Our Next Evolution *with Bill Reed*
110	**PRACTICING THE WHOLE** Moving from Ego-systems to Ecosystems *with Bill Reed*

130	**NESTED TIME ON THE BRAIN'S RIGHT SIDE**	
	Holistic Thinking, Time Management & Making Risotto	
144	**ECOLOGICAL *ORDNUNG* AND THE EVALUATION OF TECHNOLOGY**	
	Showing Restraint in an Unrestrained World	
160	**A LIVING TRANSPORTATION FUTURE**	
	Getting Around in a Regenerative Society	
174	**CHILD-CENTERED PLANNING**	
	A New Specialized Pattern Language Tool	
192	**THE POWER OF GOOD DESIGN**	
	Beauty as a Force for Change	
204	**SALVAGE MODERNISM**	
	A New Design Philosophy, Aesthetic and Ecological Approach	
216	**THE HABITAT OF HUMANITY**	
	A Wild to Clinical Continuum	
234	**BIOGRAPHY**	
	Jason F. McLennan	
236	**ABOUT**	
	International Living Future Institute, Ecotone Publishing, Living Building Challenge, McLennan Design	
237	**OTHER BOOKS BY JASON F. MCLENNAN**	

FOREWORD

by Bill Reed

Life is the process of cognition, being and becoming...[1]

Evolutionary biologist Elisabet Sahtouris has asserted that cooperation is the hallmark of a species' evolutionary trajectory. She proposes that a tendency toward competition is the marker of an immature level of biological development, occurring when a relatively new species strives to establish itself before it learns to form cooperative alliances.[2]

Young immature species are the ones that grab as much territory and resources as they can, multiplying as fast as they can. But the process of negotiations with other species matures them, thus maturing entire ecosystems. Rainforests that have evolved over millions of years are a good example. No species is in charge—the system's leadership is distributed among all species, all knowing their part in the dance, all cooperating in mutual consistency.[3]

The competing viewpoints and entry points of the early green design movement looks a lot like Ms. Sahtouris' description. I think we can all look in the mirror and see the reflection of our competitive perspectives.

My collaborative journey with Jason F. McLennan, as well as my own development, has pretty much followed this trajectory. As fellow pioneering species in the processes of working with living systems, Jason

---

1 Paraphrased from Anaïs Nin; Humberto Maturana,
2 Ben Haggard and Pamela Mang of Regenesis Group, *Regenerative Development and Design, Growing Capabilities and Practices for Co-evolving Human and Natural Systems*, to be released fall of 2016
3 Elisabet Sahtouris, *Earth Dance: Living Systems in Evolution*, LifeWeb 1999

Jason has been tremendously artful and influential in shifting the focus of the building industry to look through the lens of life in a way people can grasp from a contemporary world-view.

and I, from my perspective anyway, were mildly irritating to each other. Jason has been tremendously artful and influential in shifting the focus of the building industry to look through the lens of life in a way people can grasp from a contemporary world-view. His gift is finding just the right transformational turn of phrase or story to define a fresh entry point to awaken new possibilities regarding the human role on this planet; the Living Future Institute is an outcome of that. Our work at Regenesis, on the other hand, is based on the premise of starting with the largest, manageable, whole, and living system — a big, yet powerful bite to chew on.

From the ancient understanding of the Oneida, Paula Underwood Spencer addresses the world-view of dynamic wholeness between these poles; the place from which whole and living design can most effectively emerge.

As a part of the Native American training I received from my father, one of the aspects of perception that I was asked to understand was the distinction between Hawk and Eagle, between the way Hawk perceives and the way Eagle perceives.

When hunting, Hawk sees Mouse... and dives directly for it. When hunting, Eagle sees the whole pattern... sees movement in the general pattern... and dives for the movement, learning only later that it is Mouse. What we are talking about here is Specificity and Wholeness. Western science deals from the specific to

> **The visionary transformational thoughts in this important book demonstrate the multiple and synergistic entry points that can lead us to open up to new potentials in design and life.**

generalities about the whole. Indigenous science begins with an apprehension of the Whole, only very carefully and on close inspection reaching tentative conclusions about any Specificity.

So Hawk — the tendency to look at the Specific — and Eagle — the tendency to look at the Whole — have something to say to one another. And if they both listen, what is engendered is what is called in my tradition an Interactive Circle. Like Yin-and-Yang, each encourages the other toward heightened acuity.[4]

Of course! We are all working towards the same end. Our best possible course of action is to get off our reactive and automatic world-view and helpfully encourage each other towards heightened acuity. This journey towards wholeness is difficult, rewarding, and ultimately joyful, and it asks us to remain forever teachable.

We are now entering a new and more mature phase in the world of ecological systems thinking and design. The last three years have seen a noticeable shift in interest and willingness of developers and organizations to address all facets of life and relationships as a whole evolutionary process. This assertion is based on many conversations with clients and consultants and a review of the number of firms who are making the attempt to work with the whole system of life, not just a few specialized domains.

4 Paula Underwood Spencer, *A Native American Worldview*, From Noetic Sciences Review, Summer 1990

The visionary transformational thoughts in this important book demonstrate the multiple and synergistic entry points that can lead us to open up to new potentials in design and life. From the practice perspective of regenerative development — a topic that he and I address as co-writers in a few of the pieces in this book — Jason is shifting the purpose of design from that of designing objects and "stuff" to reconsidering the nature of human and ecological co-development. It is in engaging renewed relationships between living entities that the systemic healing, or "wholing", of our communities and places can begin.

The evolutionary leap in our role as designers — a big and essential shift in terms of the practice of sustainability — is to engage the evolutionary processes of life with a new paradigm of caring and understanding. This engagement ultimately requires shifting the purpose of our practice to work with living entities (communities, watersheds, organizations, and so on) as whole and non-reduceable organisms. To participate most effectively in this practice requires our organizations *and us* to consciously become co-evolutionary with these living wholes — *Bio-becoming* if you will; to understand and undertake our role as an integral part of these nested systems. In other words, to examine ourselves and begin the same journey as we co-create new relationships — between oneself, each other, and the powerful and healing effect we can then have in the world.

BILL REED

Explorer, Architect, Planner, Author
Regenesis Group

SO TOO CAN WE

A Poem of Regeneration

BY JASON F. MCLENNAN

Just as we cut down all the trees,
so too can we plant them back

Just as we dammed the rivers,
so too can we tear dams down

Just as we piped the streams,
so too can we bring them light

Just as we drained the ponds,
so too can we fill them back

Just as we plowed the plains,
so too can we leave them fallow

Just as we polluted the air,
so too can we filter and clean it

Just as we stripped the soil,
so too can we compost and return it life

But for those species we have lost,
forever gone, their songs are silent

So too can we mourn their loss

and honor

their passing

with

silence.

A SUSTAINED AWAKENING OF THE HUMAN HEART
LOVE AND GREEN BUILDING

A Small Musing on a Big Subject

BY JASON F. MCLENNAN

My name is Jason and I practice green building for a simple reason: a four letter word, in fact.

LOVE... the most important four-letter word there is.

Sounds corny I know but it's the truth — and I think it's the truth for many of us in the green building movement. I bet it's true for you.

Why would we do this green building thing when sometimes it can be so difficult?

Typically, we meet considerable resistance — we have to confront people who do not want to do things differently and we have to fight to make change, which sometimes feels like the opposite of love.

Often, we lose and have to compromise on the potential that we can see so clearly but can't quite reach.

We take on risks — personal and professional — and have to unlearn and relearn things when it would be so much easier to just do things "the normal way."

I know that some people do this for different reasons — for money, for market position, or because others are doing it — and this is okay as a place to begin.

But I think most people are into it for a much more fundamental reason. They may not know it or appreciate it or be aware of it, or they may be aware of it but find it uncomfortable to talk about it.

But it's the reason I do it. LOVE.

I believe that Love is at the heart of the green building movement even if that might make some people uncomfortable to say out loud.

It's good to be uncomfortable once in a while.

As cheesy as it sounds, love is a most powerful force and it is why our movement is not just a fad. It is here to stay and it's building momentum each year.

Despite what happens to the stock market and however the political winds are blowing, once someone's "lights" are turned on to green building and they have connected their heart and mind to the changes happening around us, well, –it's impossible to go back into the dark.

It's the reason why we will eventually succeed.

When you love something, you want to take care of it; to preserve it and to ensure its wellbeing through time. I love my children like that, but love can extend outwards in powerful ways beyond a love for family or to other things...

When you love a *place* you also want to take care of it; to preserve it and to ensure its well being... and you dedicate your life to that task, looking after your neighborhood or region even if you know you likely will not live to see the love bear all its fruit.

Love comes in many forms, and all can be quite powerful. That's why so many of us practice green building.

> When you love something, you want to take care of it; to preserve it and to ensure its wellbeing through time. I love my children like that, but love can extend outwards in powerful ways beyond a love for family or to other things...

This does not mean we literally love our buildings (although some are worthy of love)! But it's love that underlies the philosophy of what we are trying to do.

We know that the built environment is humanity's largest manifestation. Our largest impacts on the health of the planet are our cities and towns and the buildings and homes within them.

We understand that as we continue to add people... crossing seven billion and heading to eight billion... that these impacts are growing and expanding.

With a heavy heart we understand that all life support systems around the globe are in decline and the rate of that decline is increasing. It's a frightening trend, really.

We see with our eyes the diminishment of so many places that we love, and fear for the places that are next to be diminished or will soon disappear altogether.

It is our *love* that pushes us to sit with the pain of this reality and then to act in the ways we have at our disposal.

I do not believe that a silver bullet technology will save us — nor will a messianic politician or anything "out there." The only thing that can save us is a *sustained awakening of the human heart*.

A sustained awakening of the human heart is required to return our species to where we belong: as an essential, integral part of the beautiful, wonderful, amazement that is our planet. Not separate from the natural world, and certainly not "above it" as the dominating entity. That's not love — that's ego.

Some people get into green building for very personal reasons. They love their children and their grandchildren and they understand that leaving a healthy future to them is essential.

They now understand that the impacts that once seemed so far away *are in the here and now*, already upon us — and **we** are **that** future generation.

We recognize that old platitudes about "leaving the world in a better place for future generations" can be used as an excuse to put off action and that urgency is required.

Some people get into green building because they love their communities and the wider networks of people who surround them. They love their streets, their neighborhoods, their villages and the wonderful connections between people of all walks of life.

They see green building as a way to reconnect us to each other once again. It helps us get excited about local food, local building and local, living economies that bring us closer.

Like you, I have seen development destroy the places of my childhood — both natural and man-made. Like you, I am motivated to turn back the tide and be part of the regeneration of the land, thus blurring the distinction between the built and natural environments.

Some people get into green building because they see people suffering from health impacts related to poor indoor air quality and exposure to toxins.

They see loved ones come down with cancers that are clearly environmentally related and watch as people they care about struggle with allergies and asthma.

They realize that we are surrounded by a spew of toxic chemicals and without product transparency we cannot even know where to begin. If

It is possible to love people you'll never have a chance to meet. A love for all of humanity drives members of this movement to make change.

we don't know what's in the things we buy, how can we tell the good from the bad?

Our buildings often harbor mold and other hazards and we often "clean" them with chemicals that may only worsen our health.

I've lost too many people I love to cancer and struggled my entire life with allergies that were likely caused from pollution in my hometown — so for me it's personal. I suspect it may be for you as well.

Some people get pulled into green building because they also begin to understand that the way we design, build and operate our buildings often has hidden upstream and downstream consequences on those who are less fortunate than we.

They begin to connect the dots between the things we use and where they are made and understand that the majority of the pollution from the things we enjoy is externalized on the most economically disadvantaged; people who will never themselves enjoy the fruits of their own labor.

It is possible to love people you'll never have a chance to meet. A love for all of humanity drives members of this movement to make change.

When you dig into it, you realize that you can't have two worlds — the haves and have-nots — and expect to have a healthy future for all. Economic resilience, ecological resilience and local self-reliance are all inextricably linked.

There are economic reasons as well. Green building asks people to build using local materials and to support regional economies. Sourcing local means there is greater accountability for impacts.

Perhaps it would be good if local differences started re-emerging to celebrate the differences that should exist from place-to-place — regional design should trump a bland internationalism.

And speaking of design, some people practice green building because they have come to realize that by focusing on performance and resource conservation, they can imbue greater meaning into the design process. Better buildings result from a consideration of a larger set of critical issues.

We need to end up with a new normal; a paradigm of green buildings that are beautiful and inspiring to be around — buildings worthy of the resources they are made from.

Of course there are other people who do this because of a pure love of the wild. They love other species big and small and see the impacts we are having on habitat the world over — in our forests and swamplands, and in our oceans and streams. They understand that materials come from somewhere and toxic releases end up in unintended places. The rich biological heritage of the planet is under direct and sustained assault.

If you are like me, you are deeply and profoundly saddened by the loss of the incredible heritage of animals and plants and other creatures too small to notice.

It is sad to think that my grandchildren will likely never see a polar bear or a rhino or a tiger.

We mine, clear-cut and pollute, and then trade these resources all over the world.

> **It is sad to think that my grandchildren will likely never see a polar bear or a rhino or a tiger.**

We move from low-cost to high-cost and take from wherever environmental regulations are the most lax. We treat finite resources as if they were infinite and habitat like it can be abused forever.

Some people express their love through their faith and know that **how** we are currently living goes against the very grain of their beliefs. Can you believe in something **greater** than what we can understand without acknowledging the interconnectedness of everything?

Perhaps, just perhaps, our role is to be stewards of this creation.

Oh yes, it will take a sustained awakening of the human heart to recognize kinship with all species; to realize what we do to them we do to ourselves and to understand that this is morally wrong.

Yes, we love trees and we might be inclined to hug them (or simply to admire them if we think it unseemly to squeeze bark). We spend time in wild places when we can, and we love the feel of the rain on our face and the wind in our hair.

There are those of us who like to hunt and fish and get sustenance directly from the natural world. People who love these activities see them as an essential part of their identity, as they should. I believe hunters are more connected than people who get their food only from freezers or boxes.

Others might only hunt with cameras and chase rainbows and vistas of light and dark instead of venison or grouse. And this is okay too.

Some of us simply take comfort knowing that wildness is there… protected while we sit safely inside a responsibly made building.

We who practice green building know in our guts that paving over wetlands and forest lands — even farmland and pasture — is moving us deeply into dangerous ground and diminishing who we are as a people.

We feel the dull pain of suburbia eating the country and the endless insatiable demand for cheap goods and cheap thrills. We say no more!

Which brings us finally to a healthy love of self. To love outwardly requires a healthy love inwardly. Perhaps if more of us cared deeply for our own being, we would have the balance and perspective required to **effectively** extend that care outwards.

But the good news is that more of us awaken each year. We accept that there are things, people, places, creatures big and small that we care for passionately and that are worth fighting for.

We take up our causes because our hearts are awakened.

We join similar movements that have yet to be united, yet whose roots are equally dug deep into the soil of caring.

Much of what I'm talking about here could apply to sustainable agriculture and organic farming, or the social justice movement or local economies or environmentalism generally.

We are one movement with different areas of focus — merely different tribes of the same people — but we are all doing this from a place of love.

It is time we collaborated and united these tribes .

We need new tools, new systems and, most of all, new stories; new stories that properly frame our humanity and our civilization within a truly sustainable, regenerative future.

So we practice green building because it's an actionable way to express our love where the impacts are largest and the effects most evident — in the very places where we live and work.

We work on green buildings because it's the only responsible thing to do.

I take heart that beautiful people like you give a damn and are trying to make change regardless of how hard it may seem to be.

I appreciate it and love you for it. ■

A LIVING COMMUNITY ON EARTH

The Swelling Horde, Carrying Capacity and a Constrained World

ORIGINALLY PUBLISHED 2014

"If we don't halt population growth with justice and compassion, it will be done for us by nature, brutally and without pity and will leave a ravaged world."

Nobel Laureate
Dr. Henry W. Kendall

If it takes you about ten minutes to read this article, the global population will have increased by approximately 1500 people[1] between now and when you reach the final paragraph. The same number of humans will join the roster of earthly occupants in the ten minutes that follow. And so the pattern will continue, in the minutes, hours and days ahead, until the carrying capacity of the planet is simply overwhelmed or our population is checked in some way.

Environmentalists and scientists have always understood that we have a crisis in both overconsumption and overpopulation, yet recently it has become nearly taboo to even discuss the latter, even as we remain completely ineffective in dealing with the former.

Population control is a tricky issue. Political leaders are afraid to tackle it because it is so culturally, religiously and politically charged. The very nature of the population discussion can be extremely polarizing. Look to those who have broached the topic in the past — Malthus, Ehrlich, and others — only to be vilified and heavily criticized not just by their contemporaries but by subsequent generations as well.

Just as with issues of race, gender and other social touchstones, we typically avoid serious exploration of overpopulation because of the minefield that must be navigated to get anywhere near the topic. Meanwhile, that net-growth population clock is ticking. (Since you started reading this piece, more than 100 people have been added to the global figures.) We can't afford to wait any longer to ask and answer these fundamental questions:

- How many people can the planet sustain and at what acceptable quality of life?

- What do we do about a rising global population in an ever-constrained world when increases in population are unevenly distributed? How does rising population change as the realities of climate change and habitat disruption become more evident?

- Does one species have the right to expropriate a disproportionate amount of the planet's resources? How much of the biosphere can we claim before the system itself collapses?

- How does humanity fit within the larger web of life? What is our responsibility and our role as stewards?

---

1. www.worldpopulationbalance.org/faq (140 per minute)
   www.census.gov/population/international/files/wp02/wp-02003.pdf (141 per minute)
   www.medindia.net/patients/calculatora/worldpopulation.asp (150 per minute)

> "If the world is to save any part of its resources for the future, it must reduce not only consumption but the number of consumers."

- B.F. Skinner, *Introduction to Walden Two* (1976 edition)

HUMANS, BY THE NUMBERS

In October 1999, global population reached the six billion mark. By October 2011, only 12 years later, population had increased by a further one billion. Currently, we are nearing 7,237,700,000 people. Demographers estimate that we are on track to be eight billion strong by the spring of 2024 and that the ten-billionth human being will be born in 2062.[2]

It is impossible for us to continue this rate of growth safely and sustainably. If this is not patently obvious, then we are delusional. The planet just can't handle it; at the current rate of consumption, we are already using more than one planet's worth of renewably sustaining resources. Like locusts, we are literally eating the world and eating our future. When Malthus made his dire predictions about population in the 18th century, the world was a very different place. He did not have the benefit of an interconnected network of scientific research to guide his predictions. Population was also growing rapidly in a context of a healthy, still largely undisturbed and therefore resilient planet. The same could even be said about the state of affairs when Ehrlich published his first warnings in the 1960s, although conditions were unquestionably beginning to tip at that point. Since then, however, our species has wreaked havoc on the entire climate and on virtually every ecosystem. Because of the damage we have caused, the planet is neither healthy nor resilient. Climate change makes things increasingly unstable as droughts, shifting rain patterns, rising temperatures and ocean acidification create significant new challenges. And all the while, we continue to grow in numbers as more of the world emulates the consumption patterns of the United States and other industrialized countries.

As a global community, it is paramount that we engage in real dialogue and push the issue that there are simply too many of us. Population and consumption both should be a matter of political discussion at the national and international levels, yet our political discourse is more focused on stemming immigration, a shortsighted viewpoint that further demon-

---

2 www.worldometers.info/world-population

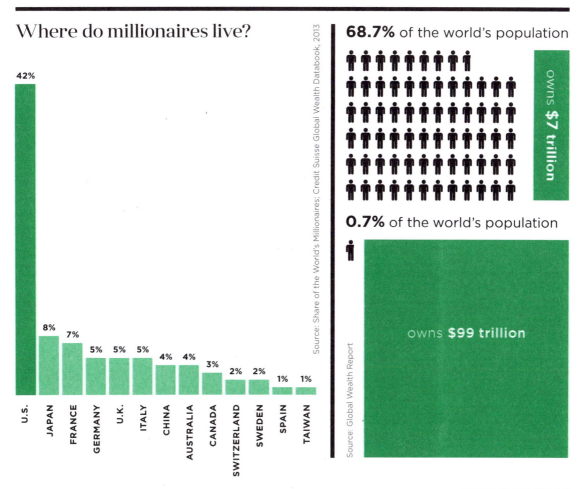

"It is an obvious truth... that population must always be kept down to the level of the means of subsistence."

- Thomas Robert Malthus, *An Essay on the Principle of Population* (1798)

strates the need for thoughtful and compassionate leadership. By truly understanding the earth's carrying capacity, based on a humane quality of living for every citizen of the planet, we can then explore rational and healthy strategies that will allow us to return to sustainable population levels elegantly, peacefully and cooperatively.

It is my belief that one of the most critical and urgent of humanity's goals should be to reach a truly sustainable population target as quickly as possible, while ensuring a humane quality of life for all. With the help of science, we can determine approximately how many people can be supported given Earth's new resource and climate reality. We already know that this means many decades of below replacement rates for most countries. In each region, for each climate and within each local economy, what is realistic? What is equitable? What is livable? What is required to preserve the beautiful web of life that sustains us all?

TAKE ONLY WHAT YOU CAN CARRY

One can't discuss global population without putting the topic in the context of the planet's ecological carrying capacity. It is universally understood that there are limits to what any environment can do to sustain the species that rely on it. A potted plant, for instance, can only draw nutrients from the finite amount of soil in that one pot. The same is true of all global species — including humans — that draw from what their natural environments can provide. We are not exempt from these fundamental laws, and yet we act as if we are.

Those who insist that Malthus was wrong — that he was nothing more than a pessimistic alarmist — tend to use his failed predictions as proof that humans can always find technological solutions to manage whatever challenges come our way. But we can't keep assuming that we can invent our way out of the problems we face. There is only so much a finite system can do to sustain us, especially one in which we've used up the majority of its failsafe reserves. Period. No present or future technological innovation will be able to protect us if we keep multiplying and keep increasing our rate of consumption.

Photo: Unsplash / Joshua K. Jackson

Not even better cities and greater urban density — a topic that is currently in fashion and one about which I have also written — can save us.[3] It is only very recently that the majority of humanity is located in cities rather than in rural locations, and this is an experiment that has yet to be adequately tested.

WHO ON EARTH IS RESPONSIBLE?

As is true with discussions surrounding climate change, we cannot allow ourselves to get sidetracked by petty arguments that pit sides — and nations — against each other. While we bicker about what is fair, just and holistically accurate, the planet continues to warm, and the future of our species becomes more tenuous. Overpopulation is a global concern, and responsibility must be shared by both developed and developing countries. A shared approach must be immediate and not tied to one group or country having to act before the other does. Rich and poor countries may need to handle their approaches differently, and certainly the economics and incentives will differ, but all parties must still be engaged. Population concerns exist regardless of geopolitical contexts.

---

3   Too many people are falling into the trap that 'cities will save us,' putting unrealistic hopes on the urbanization of the planet as a proxy for responsible resource use. While urbanization can address some issues, it creates other problems that we don't yet fully grasp.

Photo: Pixabay / StockSnap

When it comes to consumption, without a doubt the industrialized countries are by far the most serious offenders — with the United States typically leading the way on most indicators. It is estimated that the wealthiest 20 percent of the global population is responsible for 76.6 percent of total private consumption, while the poorest one-fifth among us account for only 1.5 percent of consumption.[4] Birthrates in most developed countries are declining, which is an undeniably positive trend — and interestingly enough, birth rates in many developing nations are dropping as well.[5] If developing nations continue to follow the same trend, this will begin to tip the population side of the equation in the right direction in a short amount of time. The key is to reduce both consumption and birthrates in all segments of the global community at the same time. It's a zero sum game if population drops only to see per capita consumption grow as a result.

It is unfair to suggest that developing countries bear the burden of addressing both population and consumption without help — especially since most industrialized nations owe significant portions of their prosperity to the exploitation of people in developing countries, environments and economies. Indeed, it is my belief that a global framework

4 www.globalissues.org/issue/235/consumption-and-consumerism

5 www.washingtonpost.com/blogs/wonkblog/wp/2013/05/13/why-are-birthrates-falling-around-the-world-in-a-word-television/

> "We must rapidly bring the world population under control, reducing the growth rate to zero or making it negative. Conscious regulation of human numbers must be achieved. Simultaneously we must, at least temporarily, greatly increase our food production."

\- Paul R. Ehrlich, *The Population Bomb* (1969)

around population is required and should be largely financed by developed nations as a way of elevating the immediate plight of the poor while also helping them to leapfrog over the worst stages of industrialization, which all too often is polluting, wasteful and consumer oriented.

The cell phone revolution has shown that it is possible for countries to skip over conventional technological deployment and get benefits from an industry without as much ecological and industrial impact. As poor communities develop , if they can skip immediately to renewables without stopping along the way to build natural gas, coal and nuclear infrastructure — we all benefit. If poor communities that face sanitation challenges around water and waste can skip over our obsession with indoor plumbing and flush toilets and build safe, elegant and affordable composting based systems — again all of us benefit. Our work with Living Buildings around the world has shown that it is possible to create the physical infrastructure that we need for all human activity without being tied to out-scaled resource-intensive systems that are socially and environmentally degrading.

The Challenge provides a framework not just for water, waste and energy in the built environment, but for resiliency and self-sufficiency that can help sustain people and communities alike. More importantly, it provides a guide for corrective action so that developing countries do not have to repeat the mistakes of developed countries. By offering aspirational tools such as Living Buildings and Living Communities, we can show developing countries the folly of our old ways and help them avoid some of the most brutal side effects of what we now recognize as outdated approaches. It is arrogant to suggest to developing countries that they not aspire to the level of comfort and safety that developed societies currently enjoy — Living Buildings, by being more beautiful, healthy and successful, show that leapfrogging is not a downgrade but the best idea forward.

KID STUFF

Populations grow one newborn baby at a time, so tackling the topic must be explored on both the macro (global) and the micro (household) levels. Where, then, do children and families fit into the larger discussion of population? This is where things can get pretty interesting.

Let's begin by recognizing that the cultural and social impact children have on our society — indeed, on our humanity — is priceless. I believe that children are foundational to the emotional and physical health of our communities, and it's my belief that we continue to let down our most important assets through the design of our communities. Our children keep us youthful and hopeful, while giving us a tangible reason to improve the world around us.

Still, as a global family, we need to commit to having fewer children in all nations, rich and poor.

I must acknowledge that I myself have a large family, at least by zero-population-growth standards. My wife and I have four children in our blended family, the oldest of whom I had the great privilege of meeting as a four-year-old when I met Tracy, and the youngest of whom came as a bit of a joyful surprise. Given the size of my household, some may say I am contributing to the population growth problem, especially since as Americans/Canadians we statistically consume more than anyone per capita. Perhaps I am. But I don't regret my personal decisions for a minute — my children continue to be the strongest motivator I have for the work I do in the environmental and social justice realms, and they have made my life immeasurably more enjoyable and meaningful. Who is ever to say that any specific children should not be born, or that people shouldn't want to build a family and play a role in the great and wonderful thread of life?

> **Who is ever to say that any specific children should not be born, or that people shouldn't want to build a family and play a role in the great and wonderful thread of life?**

This isn't a case of simply saying "Do as I say, not as I do"; the fact of the matter is that everyone needs to be part of the population discussion without judgment, guilt and shame — a lot of people are turned off exactly because they are positioned as part of the problem, and they automatically can't live up to some "holier than thou" standard. Too easily, topics of population lead some to propose solutions based on judgment and discrimination that bring out the worst in humanity. In the same way that past societies stigmatized people without children, population solutions are also misguided if they stigmatize people who do have children or who want more of them. Seems like a conundrum — yet I believe actually it's not.

Addressing population head-on, while respecting our innate and beautiful drive to procreate and bear wonderful, amazing children is not contradictory — it is in fact part of the magic of life.

Life is filled with issues that are not black and white, and this is one of them. My belief is that it is pressures unrelated to the biological drive to reproduce that have caused the most harmful population spikes around the world. In the majority of cases over the last century (really the only time where humans have overpopulated the earth except in small pockets), population increases in unhealthy ways due to man-made social, religious and economic inequities and injustices[6] — especially attitudes toward women and their place in society, and attitudes toward all people in situations where the few control the destiny of the many.[7] Without these larger, negative societal influences, I believe we would do fairly well as a whole at regulating our population within carrying capacity.

6 And I mean literally man-made in this case — as in constructs designed by male-dominated societies.
7 More on that in a moment.

Photo: Pixabay / drkiranhania

DOLLARS & CENTS

Some worry that a lower national birthrate could adversely affect a country's gross national product. But Japan, for one, is proving that theory wrong.[9] In spite of a shrinking population with a proportionately large senior demographic, Japan's GDP per capita is getting stronger. In the modern era that allows "workers" to stay productive well into their later years (thanks to a shift from agrarian to technology-oriented economic models), combined with advances in medical science that support healthy aging, there is less of a correlation between older demographics and GDP. Japan is teaching us that new paradigms reflecting current realities are possible. Many other of the leading GDPs in the world are countries where population rates are below replacement level.

Creating and enforcing hard and fast rules about how many children are allowed by law — legislative, religious, economic or otherwise — for any particular family is not the answer. Draconian solutions that place all the blame for overpopulation on certain segments of the population are also not the answer. China's one-child policy is a perfect example. Several decades ago, there was an understandable reaction to what the Chinese government saw as a convergence of coming social, economic and environmental crises driven largely by overpopulation. They enacted an unprecedented national policy to immediately address the situation.

On a mathematical level, the one-child initiative has been a success — China's growth rate has been greatly reduced even as the country, for a few more decades at least, continues to grow.[8] But the policy has also created some horrible side effects: gender, disability and ethnic biases; an imbalanced male-female ratio; and a potentially top-heavy demographic with too few people available to care for a disproportionately large elderly population. In recent months, the policy has been relaxed, and more exceptions have been granted for replacement rate family size. Still, this institutionalized attempt to attack the problem provides a good case study of what does and doesn't work, especially when compared to countries,

[8] It will take until approximately 2030 for China's population to peak and then slowly decline.
[9] globalpublicsquare.blogs.cnn.com/2014/01/20/is-japans-aging-population-a-good-thing

> The population problem is one of the most serious symptoms of a patriarchal society.

such as many in Europe, that did not take such actions yet have achieved similarly significant population growth rate reductions and growth rates below the replacement level of 2.1 (refer to graphic on page 33).

A WOMEN'S ISSUE

Getting serious about global population means first focusing on the plight of women and girls around the world. The places where women do not have control over their own bodies and are treated as secondary citizens to men are almost always the places where unhealthy population pressures exist. In places where women have full access to education, leadership and healthcare, birthrates have declined below the replacement rate in almost every case. In other words, the population problem is one of the most serious symptoms of a patriarchal society.

Too often, patriarchy-based religious beliefs push women to have more children than they want or can safely take care of. When they are educated and empowered,[10] women as a whole make the smartest demographic and family planning decisions possible.[11]

Women, who carry the largest burden of bearing and raising children, are best equipped to make the majority of decisions in this area — and men, after centuries of abysmal decision making in this area, should cede leadership.

So, ironically, the best solution for population control is not to impose restrictions on birth — but to eliminate restrictions on women's rights and reproductive health.

TOO MUCH TO ASK

There are those who say that humans and the planet are adaptable; that we could never starve the environment to the point of starving ourselves; that we will find new food sources if things get so crowded here on Earth that we run out of the things we've always relied on. Bugs are full of protein; we can eat them, they say. All is well.

10 www.earth-policy.org/data_highlights/2011/highlights13
11 www.un.org/News/Press/docs/2011/pop994.doc.htm

Measuring the Global Gender Gap: Best and Worst Countries in the World to be a Woman

The metrics of the Gender Gap Index measure gaps rather than levels, capture gaps in output variables rather than input variables and rank countries according to gender equality rather than women's empowerment. The Four Fundamental Categories of the index are: Economic Participation & Opportunity, Educational Attainment, Health & Survival and Political Empowerment.

Due to lack of sufficient data, a country must have data available for at least 12 of the 14 indicators that comprise the Four Fundamental Categories. A total of 136 countries were measured. Source: The Global Gender Gap Report, World Economic Forum, 2013

 BELOW REPLACEMENT RATE 2.1 Children/Family

 ABOVE REPLACEMENT RATE 2.1 Children/Family

20 BEST COUNTRIES (2013 rankings)

RANK	COUNTRY	BIRTH RATE total births per woman
1.	Iceland	2.0
2.	Finland	1.8
3.	Norway	1.9
4.	Sweden	1.9
5.	Philippines*	3.1
6.	Ireland	2.0
7.	New Zealand	2.1
8.	Denmark	1.7
9.	Switzerland	1.5
10.	Nicaragua*	2.5
11.	Belgium	1.8
12.	Latvia	1.4
13.	Netherlands	1.7
14.	Germany	1.4
15.	Cuba	1.5
16.	Lesotho	3.1
17.	South Africa	2.4
18.	U.K.	1.9
19.	Austria	1.4
20.	Canada	1.6

20 WORST COUNTRIES (2013 rankings)

RANK	COUNTRY	BIRTH RATE total births per woman
136.	Yemen	4.2
135.	Pakistan	3.3
134.	Chad	6.4
133.	Syria	3.0
132.	Mauritania	4.7
131.	Côte d'Ivoire	4.9
130.	Iran, Islamic Rep.	1.9
129.	Morocco	2.7
128.	Mali	6.9
127.	Saudi Arabia	2.7
126.	Benin	4.9
125.	Egypt, Arab Rep.	2.8
124.	Algeria	2.8
123.	Lebanon	1.5
122.	Oman	2.9
121.	Nepal	2.4
120.	Turkey	2.1
119.	Jordan	3.3
118.	Ethiopia	4.6
117.	Fiji	2.6

*Anomalies in the top ten are countries with strong religious pressures pushing for large families and against family planning measures.

Sources: The Global Gender Gap Report, World Economic Forum, 2013; "Fertility rate, total (births per woman)," World Development Indicators, The World Bank, 2012

But all is not well. New food sources do not justify a human population that continues to swell beyond the bounds of sustainability. Nothing does. It's a zero-sum game. No matter how much energy and resources we conserve per capita, we are sunk if the "capita" keep growing.

> I brought you into a fertile land to eat its fruit and rich produce. But you came and defiled my land and made my inheritance detestable.
>
> Jeremiah 2:7

Overpopulation is neither a developed or developing world problem. It's a human problem. A messy, enormous, complicated human problem. Children are a beautiful, essential part of why it's worth being human, and any solutions put forward must honor and support their well-being. Perhaps more tragic than the lack of attention paid to overpopulation is the lack of attention to the health and security of the children that are born each year in this world. We must take care of what we have, while we take care of how many we have.

Yet clearly there are simply too many of us, and every nation in the world must find its path to below replacement levels as soon as possible. Too many of any one species in any environment creates an imbalance within the web of life. We are no different. Nature, in its wisdom, always works to correct systems that are out of balance. My hope is that we, in our wisdom, can see the need to address population with ideas and policies of leadership before brutal corrections happen regardless of our intentions. ■

LIVING COMMUNITIES OF THE FUTURE

ORIGINALLY PUBLISHED (WITH THE TITLE "CITIES ARE NOW")
IN THE WINTER 2015 ISSUE OF *YES! MAGAZINE*

The gleam of an heroic Act

Such strange illumination

The Possible's slow fuse is lit

By the Imagination.

Emily Dickinson

If there's one thing that's certain, it's that the future hasn't happened yet. How we will live a few decades from now is anything but clear, despite predictions from our wisest architects, planners, politicians, philosophers, futurists, and science fiction writers.

For anyone committed to creating a more sustainable and just culture, here's a sobering exercise: Try looking into the past as a way of tracking society's expectations for itself. Look back a few decades and see how yesterday's visionaries predicted we'd be living now. I must do this routinely in my work in setting standards and developing tools for change at the International Living Future Institute. So I can tell you a common thread weaves through most fictionalized, artistic, and scientific forecasts: that the ongoing march of technological progress will continue unabated, further mechanizing our experience as humans and separating us from nature until everything we need is provided by machines and computers whose intelligence surpasses that of their operators. A companion theme in futuristic prophecies is the subjugation and taming of nature or, in extreme cases, nature's total elimination. In these depictions, there is little room for non-human life.

Think for a moment about the sheer bulk of stories you've read and movies you've seen, and how many of them warn of a bleak future for society — books such as Aldous Huxley's *Brave New World* and Cormac McCarthy's *The Road*, and a catalogue of dystopian cinema: Metropolis, Blade Runner, Road Warrior, Terminator, and Wall-E, just to begin the short list. The current epidemic of zombies chasing after us through our popular culture is, I think, nothing less than a psychological manifestation of our species' sense of worthlessness. The undead trudge through our cities consuming us like a cancer. What better symbol of hopelessness and lack of self-worth could we possibly conjure up?

After World War II, there was a brief age of technological optimism. People, particularly Americans, believed in the promise of new fron-

> Chicago's Cabrini Green and St. Louis' Pruitt-Igoe (both public housing projects) mimicked Le Corbusier's model only to be torn down after a few decades because the living conditions in these concrete environments grew so dreadful.

tiers. We saw residential and commercial potential in everything from our emerging suburbs to our rising office towers — we even pictured ourselves living "soon" on the moon or in terraformed space colonies.

In the mid-20th century, we were suddenly (and curiously) willing to dump models of living and community that had worked well for hundreds of years in favor of these new ideas. We raced to build an automobile-dependent world, lined with interstates and freeways that would provide the straightest path toward the idealized future. Usually these new freeways carved through our least affluent neighborhoods, separating rich from poor — and typically, black from white. It is tragic that many of our first and largest social experiments in reshaping community were conducted in disadvantaged communities, most often populated by African American residents. Most of these social experiments supplanted viable working communities with "new urban visions" that increased crime and diminished community bonds. It should not be lost on us that planning paradigms have often tested ideas on the poorest among us, only to reinforce race and class distinctions once the polished plans are eventually implemented.

Many famous architects of the last century proposed plans for communities that, while well-intentioned at the time, had seriously negative outcomes. In 1924, architect and planner Le Corbusier unveiled his Radiant City, a proposal to bulldoze the heart of Paris and replace it with tall, monolithic towers — something Paris wisely ignored. Unfortunately, his ideas gained traction in American planning circles, and cities here lacked the wisdom of French city planners. Chicago's Cabrini Green and St. Louis' Pruitt-Igoe (both public housing projects) mimicked Le Corbusier's model only to be torn down after a few decades because the living conditions in these concrete environments grew so dreadful. Frank Lloyd Wright's Broadacre City concept, which in the 1950s pictured "people living in parks connected by highways," brought us the decentralized sprawl that now mars our landscapes, separates people from the natural world, and discourages healthy walkable communities.

Photo: Flickr Creative Commons / Paul Knittel

Meanwhile, no positive, ecologically grounded conception of the future has been presented convincingly to counter these assumptions in our collective consciousness. Most futurists, whether basing their predictions on fact or fiction, seem so focused on techno-marvels they omit resilient environments and healthy communities from the stories they proffer. As a result, a more pessimistic, less natural set of mythologies has shaped our default assumptions about where we seem to be headed.

We have grown used to imagining an increasingly mechanistic future, with greater and greater densities, but what we have forgotten is that a future that crowds out the natural world is not simply bleak. It is impossible. A world without a healthy and vibrant natural biosphere cannot sustain human life.

DEBUNKING THE "INEVITABLE"

Despite what the commercial real-estate industry or science-fiction authors might want us to imagine, our future does not have to be defined exclusively by megacities, mile-high skyscrapers, machines that do everything for us, and hyperdensity filled with flying cars. This "culture of inevitability," defined by popular culture as well as market-driven development — despite being an imaginary concept — lulls us into inaction because it can seem futile to resist something so inescapable.

Remember: The future hasn't happened yet. With enough people, wisdom, and ideas it's possible to resist the culture of inevitability. We've done remakings of cities, towns, cultures, religions, governments, and more. We changed every community in America after World War II from ones that functioned primarily around walking and streetcars, to ones that function to serve automobiles. Now, clearly, it is time to switch to a more resilient paradigm. Human behavior is shaped in large part by our ability to pursue what we can imagine.

The task before us now is to harness the power of imagination to create a different future — one of our own choosing, and one crafted to sustain our communities, ourselves, and the other creatures with which we share this planet.

REIMAGINING A MORE LIVABLE FUTURE

The Human Revolution

To take control of our next evolution, we must embrace and prioritize what it means to be human; what it means to live in concert with nature. Creating a truly living community will mean changing our role on — and as a part of — the planet. It starts by reimagining our role as a species — not as separate from and superior to others, but inextricably linked to all other life and with a profound purpose as steward or gardener, helping to ensure that each act of our doing creates a net positive benefit to the greater web of life.

Instead of Homo sapiens we become (a term I have coined) Homo regenesis. Homo regenesis, which suggests moving beyond our current state as Homo sapiens, is suggestive of our next evolution to a state of being with a profound love of life; an affection for and affinity with living organisms and natural systems that is prioritized over a fondness for technology and mechanized systems. Understanding Homo regenesis means understanding the fundamental truth that only life can create conditions for life.

The Building Revolution

Next we'll need to build models of the future we seek — now. My organization, the International Living Future Institute, has been pushing the Living Building Challenge as an essential framework for all new buildings. With the Living Building Challenge we are proving it is possible to build within the carrying capacity of any given ecosystem — building struc-

Photo: Nic Lehoux

The Bullitt Center is a symbol of a revolution in modern architecture: bigger than the majority of buildings in the United States, yet free from the burden and legacy of fossil fuels in the country's least sunny major city.

tures that are completely powered by renewable energy, working within the water balance of a given site, treating their own waste, and doing so with materials that are non-toxic and local.

The Bullitt Center in Seattle is one such model — a six-story office building completely powered by the sun when averaged over the course of the year, with composting toilets on all six levels. The Bullitt Center is a symbol of a revolution in modern architecture: bigger than the majority of buildings in the United States, yet free from the burden and legacy of fossil fuels in the country's least sunny major city. Throughout the world, living schools, parks, homes, offices, and museums are cropping up in a variety of climate zones against various political backdrops. Currently more than 200 of these transformative buildings are taking shape in communities as far flung as New Zealand, China, Mexico, Brazil, and in nearly every U.S. state. If these diverse projects can achieve Living Building Challenge goals, there is no limit to how broadly we can apply these systems. Because we now have the technology to build truly regenerative communities, it is no longer a stretch to imagine the "living" paradigm as the new normal.

The Scale Revolution

Another relevant topic in the context of this discussion is something I call the "Boundary of Disconnect." I define the Boundary of Disconnect as any system's metaphysical and tactile boundary at which the individual (or any species or colony of species) is no longer able to connect or relate to the totality of the system itself. This concept is all about scale, and how we as humans should best live and relate to each other within the communities we build. In our current model of the built environment, we typically develop without heeding scale, or build slavishly to the scale of the automobile. We binge on materials, energy, and water, climbing higher and sprawling farther without considering the natural, social, or emotional consequences. But if we were smarter about the appropriate scales for our systems — building, agriculture, transportation — we would minimize problems that arise from disconnectedness. As the writer Richard Louv put it: When density is disproportionate to nature and we are disconnected from our earthly surroundings, we succumb to "nature deficit disorder."

> **The good news is that a child-centered city is not simply generous; it's practical. And what nurtures small people often helps our elders as well.**

When it comes to scale, a powerful litmus test for any community is its ability to support and nurture children. Child-centered planning would focus on our most precious and delicate citizens. It would heed the advice of Enrique Peñalosa, a former mayor of Bogotá, Colombia, who wrote, "Children are a kind of indicator species. If we can build a successful city for children, we will have a successful city for all people."

The good news is that a child-centered city is not simply generous; it's practical. And what nurtures small people often helps our elders as well. For starters (this is a very incomplete list) we would: Involve children in local food production. Sprinkle bike racks, sport courts, public art, and natural playgrounds throughout the city. Eliminate poisonous substances from the built environment. Design sheltered public waiting areas. Install swings designed for all ages across the metropolis. Create "sound parks" powered by fountains, wind chimes, drums, and live-music performanc-

> Ultimately, Living Communities of the future are both scaled to the human dimension and include functioning ecological systems throughout, where greater biodiversity and resilience can occur.

es that amplify the music of nature. Scatter courtyards linked to public spaces that offer acoustic and visual privacy from the street. Get rid of most advertising.

Even if more and more people are moving to cities, we can design streets, sidewalks, and pathways at a scale that is safe and pleasant when experienced by someone under four feet tall rather than designing everything around the scale of 3000-pound automobiles. We can design neighborhood features that support child development through welcoming natural systems such as flowing water, trees, and a myriad of ways for children to interact with the living world rather than merely being presented with a lifeless concrete jungle.

The Living Community Revolution

Ultimately, Living Communities of the future are both scaled to the human dimension and include functioning ecological systems throughout, where greater biodiversity and resilience can occur. Instead of flying cars and moon colonies, Living Communities will be filled with ultra-efficient, nontoxic Living Buildings that generate their own energy onsite using renewable resources, capture and treat their own water, are made of nontoxic sustainably sourced materials, and inspire their inhabitants. But only if we start imagining and insisting now.

The game-changing success of the Living Building Challenge is proof that Living Communities are feasible within a fabric that supports strong social and cultural networks. As we imagine and then build examples of this new paradigm, it is essential that we do not use our most economically disadvantaged as guinea pigs. Indeed, the human dimension of our cities must be carefully considered as we go forward to overcome the legacy of racial and economic prejudice that has pervaded city planning in the past.

Perhaps in the future, popular books and films will portray how we overcame mind-numbing odds and defeated the seemingly unstoppable Culture of Inevitability, and instead embraced a new vision for the way we will live on the planet — one that puts people and life squarely where they belong: at the heart of our communities. ■

PASSING THROUGH THE BOTTLENECK

Humanity's Final Gamble

ORIGINALLY PUBLISHED 2015

"Biological diversity is messy. It walks, it crawls, it swims, it swoops, it buzzes. But extinction is silent, and it has no voice other than our own."

Paul Hawken

Like most people, I have good days and bad days. When it comes to looking at the future and thinking about the pressing social and environmental issues before us, it is easy to vacillate between hopefulness and hopelessness, optimism and pessimism. If you are paying attention, it is impossible not to feel agonizing despair when looking at the convergence of global challenges such as population growth and consumption levels, habitat and species decline, and the multiple negative impacts underway with global climate change. It is very possible to imagine a future scenario where the requirements for human civilization can't be supported and life as we know it greatly diminishes — it is possible that humanity's days are numbered.

But it is impossible not to feel optimistic when witnessing the incredible innovations and emergence of cutting-edge designs, ideas, projects and technologies to make our world a better place due to the outstanding work championed by amazing people and organizations all over the world. These examples instill hope that a truly living future is possible — a world where humanity fully participates in the beautiful cycle of regeneration in which all other species are currently involved. Historically, humans did participate in this cycle, but we must reconcile our role as stewards and a keystone species.

A mature and nuanced way to deal with this is to be able to sit with the following seemingly contradictory feelings — accepting the gravity of the current environmental disturbances while maintaining hope. Losing hope has few benefits and only increases the likelihood of the first scenario of a pessimistic future of humanity coming true. Existing in hope without acknowledgement of the real possibility of human decline is at best living in delusion and at worst supports the lack of responsibility and accountability that comes from believing that someone else will save us, while we continue to consume and live within the industrial and societal framework that is the cause of the global environmental decline.

While it's easier to view the world and thoughts of the future in black-and-white terms — succumbing fully to either vision of the future — it is more mature to sit somewhere in the middle and acknowledge that the future has not yet been written while working our asses off to ensure that the positive living future is what we pass on to future generations.

Let's explore both sides of this duality.

THE DARK SIDE: TRENDS THAT FUEL HOPELESSNESS

There are a number of global trends that should cause everyone great concern about the future. For the sake of this summary, I'm not even acknowledging potential catastrophes that are beyond our control, such as meteor impacts or supernovas capable of wiping out the planet with little to no notice. There are numerous scenarios that could conceivably end us, but it does little good to dwell on those — let's save them for Hollywood action movies. It is important to acknowledge that all of the issues below are so heavily interconnected that it is hard to separate them.

1. Population and Consumption Trends

I have written previously about the exponentially increasing population which places immense strain on the planet's carrying capacity. Not only are there too damn many of us — more than seven billion humans are squeezed onto the earth, and population is projected to be eight-billion strong by 2024[1] — but we appropriate too much of the earth's resources to support ourselves. To make matters worse, consumption trends are increasing at an unhealthy pace, especially as developing countries begin to emulate the typical behavior of westernized countries' reliance and overconsumption of natural resources. According to one estimate, worldwide private consumption expenditures have increased four-fold in the last half-century.[2]

2. Climate Change

While debate continues regarding the precise timing and severity of global climate change, there is undeniable evidence that the earth is warming at an alarming rate. Prior to the Industrial Revolution, natural causes (such as variations in how the sun's energy reached Earth and changes in the planet's atmospheric reflectivity) were largely to blame. However, the responsibility for climate change in the modern age — including the dramatic warming that has occurred in the past 75 years — falls squarely on human shoulders.[3] Accordingly, in the coming decades, we should expect to see even more dramatic weather shifts, natural disasters, droughts, ocean acidification, disappearing glaciers, melting ice caps, and rising sea levels.

3. Famine, Drought and War

Climate change leads to food and water shortages, ecosystem diebacks, nutrient scarcity and hunger. Left unchecked, these conditions spread from microclimates to regions, ultimately threatening the stability of

---

1   www.worldometers.info/world-population
2   www.worldwatch.org/node/810

> "Lord save us all from old age and broken health and a hope tree that has lost the faculty of putting out blossoms." - Mark Twain

global food supplies and contributing to further desertification and resource challenges. History has shown that ecological crises typically raise questions about who has the right to Earth's natural resources, particularly when they are in short supply. How will we feed our population (especially in regions already stretched thin by poverty and hunger) when water and soil are precious commodities? How will we deal with vast numbers of climate refugees who become displaced?

4. Global Pandemics

The 2014 Ebola outbreak demonstrated how quickly illness can spread when international travel allows infected individuals to cross the globe in a matter of hours. The recent rash of measles only helped prove the point of how infectious diseases can become easily widespread with modern day travel. Yet imagine what is possible with something as highly transmittable and deadly as smallpox. As population numbers and densities climb, and as we are ever-more connected through a network of international airports, it doesn't take long to envision certain infectious diseases spreading faster than they can be vaccinatated or treated. The consequences are potentially deadly. Then, once bacteria develop resistance to the antibiotics, the cycle starts anew. The age of antibiotics is perhaps coming to a scary end as even small skin infections can now turn deadly again.

5. Diminished Global Resilience from Habitat and Species Loss

A healthy natural world is fundamental to the survival of all species. The more we degrade or destroy natural habitats, the greater the risk of species extinction. The World Wildlife Fund claims that habitat loss is the primary threat to 85 percent of all at-risk species.[4] Human activities alter and sometimes eradicate entire ecosystems through the relentless pursuit of goods and services. This process of habitat elimination systematically threatens thousands of interdependent species, which makes everything

---

4 wwf.panda.org/about_our_earth/species/problems/habitat_loss_degradation/

less resilient to further disruptions. If honeybees become extinct, for example, they'll take their pollinating capabilities with them, so fruits and nuts may not be far behind.[5] The more compromised global habitat diversity becomes, the greater the likelihood of species extinction and cascading effects that could ultimately undermine our very existence, given that humanity ultimately relies on thousands of other species for its survival and certainly for its well-being. So just as we are making the world less stable due to climate change, we are also undermining the very systems that could help us adapt.

6. Nuclear Disaster

The 2011 Fukushima Daiichi meltdown demonstrates that even the most sophisticated safeguards aren't powerful enough to withstand the effects of a nuclear accident. With nuclear power present in more than two dozen countries (and nuclear weapons in at least nine[6]) the potential for catastrophe is very real — coupled with the potential for increased terrorist activity, humanity currently rests in a very precarious position. However, even simple human error — a cause for past nuclear disasters — is equally as dangerous. Any technology that requires constant vigilance for future generations is immoral and dangerous.

7. Technological Singularity and the Lack of Human Purpose

Some researchers hypothesize that our technological innovations will one day progress to the point where artificial intelligence will exceed human brainpower, ultimately taking over civilization and relegating the human species to subservience...or worse. I tend to think this is very unlikely, but the concern itself is an important reflection of an existential crisis I believe humanity is experiencing. It's not outrageous to question whether we will be rendered obsolete by machines, as this is already happening on a number of levels: grocery store checkouts, manufacturing and the use and capabilities of software, to name a few. Whether the contribution of human physical and intellectual labor will become obsolete in the modern industrial world is very real — leaving us potentially without purpose and with too much time on our hands — a dangerous combination.

---

5 www.huffingtonpost.com/evaggelos-vallianatos/honeybees-on-the-verge-of_b_4326226.html
6 www.icanw.org/the-facts/nuclear-arsenals/

THE LIGHT SIDE: SEEDS OF HOPE EMERGING

Among the encouraging innovations picking up speed around the world are the following promising examples, each of which instills a dash of hope that there's still time to change our trajectory:

1. Rapid Rise of Renewable Energy and the End of the Fossil Fuel Era

We are on the cusp of an energy revolution driven by renewables. The cost per kilowatt hour of clean options (with solar at the top of the list) continues to fall, which allows these sustainable solutions to compete more directly with traditional fossil fuels despite their subsidies. According to the International Renewable Energy Agency, solar energy from photovoltaics is leading the cost decline of all sources of renewables, with the cost of PV modules falling 75 percent since the end of 2009, and the cost of electricity from utility-scale solar PV falling 50% since 2010.[7] In spite of a recent sudden drop, which likely has political underpinnings,

---

7   www.irena.org/News/Description.aspx?NType=A&mnu=cat&PriMenuID=16&CatID=84&News_ID=386

Living Buildings are now emerging all around the world — in every climate zone and every building type — rapidly showing that a new paradigm is possible for how we live and work.

petroleum prices will continue to increase in parallel with renewable energy affordability. As soon as renewables become consistently the least expensive alternative, they will dominate the energy market — quickly and completely. In fact, this change may come about sooner rather than later. The fossil fuel divestment movement is gaining steam, aided by the recent Global Divestment Day held in February, 2015. Meanwhile, even in such notoriously polluted regions as China, there is growing awareness of the need for change in demand for renewable solutions.[8]

2. Living Buildings, Living Communities

With Living Buildings and net zero energy structures developing around the globe, we are gradually creating a more sustainable built environment; the change is slow, but evident. One need only look at the Bullitt Center in Seattle, WA — a six-story, 52,000-square-foot commercial office Living Building that generates its own power and treats its own water without a drop of fossil fuels — to see what's possible. If a Class A office building in the cloudiest city in the lower 48 states can operate without fossil fuels while retaining marketability, then virtually anything is possible in the built environment, anywhere in the world. Living Buildings are now emerging all around the world — in every climate zone and every building type — rapidly showing that a new paradigm is possible for how we live and work.

3. Super-efficient Consumer Products

The advent of energy-conscious goods, from household appliances to electric cars, indicates that the consumer marketplace is ready and willing to embrace smarter choices. Just as Tesla Motors has proven that vehicles do not require combustion engines to deliver performance and elegance, brands across numerous product categories are simultaneously emerging as emblems of what is possible. Nest made a smart thermostat sexy. Comfy is changing our relationship with heating and cooling through learning from occupant behavior. Countless innovations are emerging every day. The Living Future Institute launched the Living Product

---

8 www.powerengineeringint.com/articles/2015/02/china-s-anti-pollution-strategy-drives-increased-renewable-power-demand.html

Challenge (living-future.org/lpc) in 2014 as a call for all manufacturers to produce goods that support a living future.

A huge movement in support of buying local and organic is changing consumer expectations as well. Rising demand for greener, locally manufactured products will help realign toward positive environmental and social progress.

4. People-centric Communities

As we near the end of the fossil fuel era, a greater number of neighborhoods and cities are investing in infrastructure that supports people rather than automobiles. Clean public transportation options are becoming more plentiful, and our urban centers are becoming more walkable — people are moving out of the suburbs and into the cities — vastly shrinking their ecological footprint in the process.

5. Sustainable Food Production Practices

The rise of organic food availability and a growing resistance to processed and genetically modified foods are taking us in a healthy direction. People are eating less red meat, and vegetarian and vegan diets are becoming more common. Even the shift from meat to insects offers a wonderful example of a possible positive menu change.[9] With the livestock industry responsible for more greenhouse gas emissions than the transportation industry, more people are turning away from beef, chicken and pork, and choosing different options. A combination of hard work and good policy might strengthen the sustainable food movement to the point where it can meet the demands of a growing global population while retaining nimbleness and nutritional integrity in the world's food supplies.

6. Slowing Birth Rates.

Although global population numbers continue to rise, the actual pace of new births has begun to slow and is expected to keep doing so — perhaps even reaching the point of zero growth within our lifetimes (it took 12 years to increase from 5 to 6 billion inhabitants, but 13 more years to go from 6 to 7 billion.[10] The list of nations experiencing negative population growth is increasing. Japan and Italy, for example, have been included in recent lists of nations with declining population rates, which some sources attribute to more broadly available contraception and a more empowered female demographic.[11] Declining or replacement

---

9 edibug.wordpress.com/why-eat-bugs-2/

10 www.slate.com/articles/technology/future_tense/2013/01/world_population_may_actually_start_declining_not_exploding.html

11 www.dw.de/impact-of-japans-shrinking-population-already-palpable/a-18172873 and www.lifesitenews.com/news/italian-birth-rate-continues-to-sink-and-drag-down-italian-life-satisfactio

birthrates are increasingly common in developed countries — those that also tend to have the largest per-capita environmental footprint.

7. Education and Communication

Technology has effectively created a global open-source classroom that is spreading information that can enrich and strengthen nations. Innovations in devices and connectivity give us a sense of power we've never before realized. We watch events unfold in real time from halfway around the world, which allows us to react and get involved, whether to help, participate or simply celebrate. We can interact and empathize with people and cultures that we previously never had the opportunity to encounter. There is great promise in living in an era where everyone, regardless of economic status, can carry the internet in their pockets and be connected to a global community — allowing people opportunities to self-organize, stay current on issues and connect to rapid changes. New ways of communication and more powerful communication mediums offer hope that many people can't be kept in the dark about issues that are important to their rights and survival.

8. Women's Rights

Women around the world are gaining societal ground through great strides being made to increase educational, healthcare and leadership opportunities. Gender equality strengthens the global community's chance to thrive — for too long, the majority of nations (both governmentally and socially) have operated under a patriarchy. Countries where women's rights are most tenuous are often those with the most internal strife, violence and conflict.

9. The New Story

Hope stems, too, from enthusiastic new generations coming together and facing these challenges head-on, accepting responsibilities for the present and future health of the planet in ways their predecessors were unable and/or unwilling to do. In The Great Turning, David Korten describes how there is a growing number of people who are abandoning "the old story" and readily replacing it with a new paradigm that seeks to restore a healthy connection between humanity and the natural world — a system supportive of community rather than exploitation. This growing shift is documented in my book *Zugunruhe* and touched on in "Living Communities of the Future" in this book. A shift to a new positive paradigm will require people who are self aware and recognize the need for change — each day I have the pleasure to meet individuals who are dedicated to this migration.

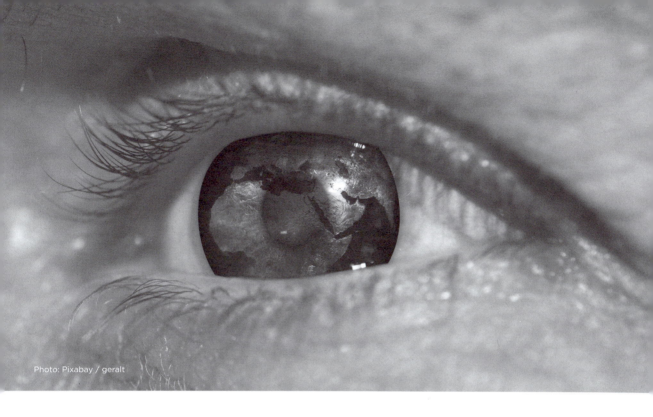

Photo: Pixabay / geralt

THE GREAT RACE — FOR HUMANITY

Given both the dark and light trends in front of us, what does this mean when mapped along a timeline? If we had all the time in the world, I'm sure the greater opportunities of hope would certainly prevail, but if we did, then we also wouldn't have to worry about the consequences of our slow rate of change. A responsible analysis must always contain a time dimension. Given where we are today and the current trajectories, and given what science is telling us, how do things really look?

We have placed ourselves in a great race to survive the consequences of our own actions — a wanton disregard for land, resources and life may have permanently diminished the environmental infrastructure necessary to sustain human life. Our consumptive tendencies may very well end up being the death of us.

But not the death of all living things.

If the human race were to disappear, the planet would undoubtedly go on. In fact, it would likely thrive and rebound more quickly than any scenario where we become much better stewards of the planet. In his book, *The World Without Us*, Alan Weisman explores how Earth would respond in the absence of people. He theorizes that it wouldn't take long for the planet to rebound and reinvent itself once it was rid of us. Mod-

From the Boundary of Disconnect to the Homo sapien Bottleneck

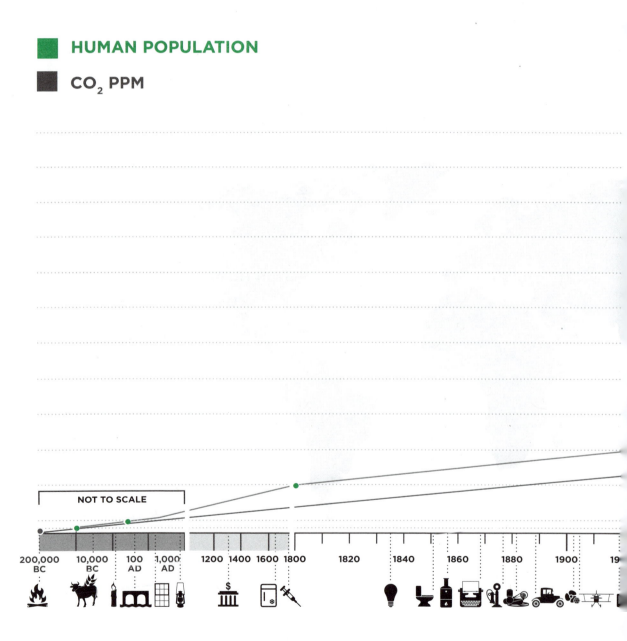

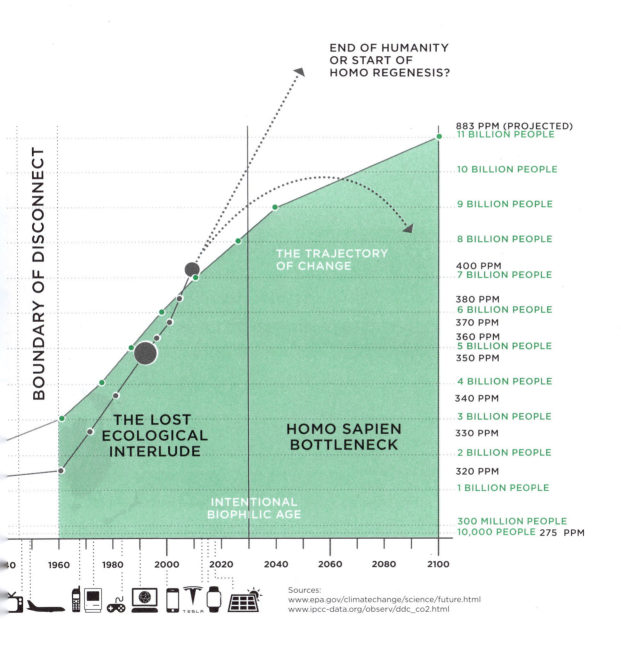

ern humans act like an invasive species. It's a sobering thought that all of the ecosystems that were here before humanity entered the industrial age would benefit from our extinction. But that's dwelling on a perverse form of hopelessness — I'd rather imagine us making it. Humanity is capable of surviving, and I think we are also worthy of it. While our actions are often deplorable and our negative impact widespread, we are capable of extraordinary beauty, love, empathy, artistic expression — and ecological sensitivity. We are capable of truly becoming Homo regenesis[12] — a species that purposefully acts to create greater positive conditions for all of life.

THE CHOKE POINT

Which trends will pull ahead and within what timeframe? Will we manage to solve these critical environmental and social issues in time to protect ourselves from extinction or massive die-off? Or have we wreaked so much havoc that our mistakes are irreparable? Are we facing an evolution to homo regenesis or the end of *Homo sapiens*?

Will we dump fossil fuels and switch to a renewable world in time for humans and earth to thrive?

We are most likely approaching a theoretical bottleneck, a point in time when human civilization either transforms or disappears. We'll either pass through or be pinched back. With every passing month, year and decade of inactivity and denial, the consequences of our choices become more serious. We can't continue to behave as we have — disregarding the damage and continuing the trends of consumption and impact. Because nature will reset, disregarding us.

In the January 2013 issue of *Trim Tab* magazine, I laid out a timeline called the Boundary of Disconnect, which depicts historic shifts in technology that allowed humans to nearly completely separate from nature in day-to-day existence. The argument is that sometime between the end of World War II and the 1960s, we crossed an invisible boundary in terms of population and planet-wide impact and entered a new age where we had to either intentionally realign how we do nearly everything, or suffer tragic consequences at some point in the next few decades. Here, I refine the graphic further with new categorizations of importance. Looking

> **It's a sobering thought that all of the ecosystems that were here before humanity entered the industrial age would benefit from our extinction. But that's dwelling again in a perverse form of hopelessness – I'd rather imagine us making it.**

---

12 To see the article in its entirety, visit www.pageturnpro.com/Cascadia-Green-Building-Council/48027-Trim-Tab-v16/index.html#1.

again at the trends in front of us, I map both the positive and negative scenarios on the timeline.

Currently, we are residing in a period of time that I call the **Lost Ecological Interlude** — a period that will either continue to be marked with further lack of progress (coupled with more marked global environmental and societal side effects of our collective decision-making) or rapid positive change due to some or all of the positive trends highlighted in this article. This is of course the period we are in now — either the greatest blowout in our planet's history — or, more positively, the beginning of the shift — what David Korten calls "the great turning." One could peg the start of this period at the late 1960s to early 1970s with the beginning of the environmental movement to perhaps sometime in the 2030s. During this time it's been possible to live and deny the reality of the quandary we are in (as so many have done) while increasing numbers of people become aware of the situation, but as the end of this short era comes to a close (likely in less than two decades) the dire situation will be impossible for anyone to ignore regardless of political bent — climate change and population pressures will ensure that.

Finally, we reach the *Homo sapien Bottleneck*, which will extend to sometime between 2030 and possibly 2100. Most likely this will be a period of incredible upheaval, the likes of which we have never seen and will be the most challenging period that humanity has ever faced. How we transition through this bottleneck (or if we will) will be directly proportional to the scale of our intervention and course correction, changing our ways in countries around the world. To date, our society hasn't done very well with change when the implications for the change are distant in the future. We react well to immediate threats — and very poorly to long-term, systemic threats. But during the Homo sapien Bottleneck period, what was once "far off" will be a daily struggle and a challenge that will confront even the wealthiest among us. Change will be demanded with more immediate repercussions.

LOSS AS A MOTIVATOR

There is a very powerful human emotion that, while sad to point out, could very well work in our favor as we approach the bottleneck: grief and direct loss. Pondering very viscerally about what we have to lose could very well spur the compassion to take action that is critical to our own survival. We have been living in the Anthropocene for some time — losing species and habitat at alarming rates for many decades — but the losses have been largely distant, abstract threats for most in developed countries. Yet the distance between us and palpable loss is shortening, and what we will be confronted with will be evident to all in the coming decades.

Consider the incredible sense of loss we'll feel when nearly every major large mammal becomes extinct. What will we tell ourselves and our children when the last of the rhinos, giraffes, lions, polar bears, tigers, hippos, gorillas and many more actually disappear forever, as they are likely to do? What happens when the rainforest does disappear completely and the rains go with it? What happens when drought comes to a huge region in the heartland — and doesn't leave?

For most citizens of developed countries, such reports are bothersome but not fully real. We tend to watch environmental and biological depletions from a distance, which protects us from internalizing the loss the way we do when a loved one dies. We can turn off the channel and look away for only so long.

The bottleneck, though, will make loss evident to people in every corner of the world at an incredible magnitude. Species loss is just one indicator. All nations will be affected — though the poorest nations will continue to be the hardest hit, which will make the effects more immediate — profound changes will affect even those of us who have previously been blissfully detached.

Environmental harm will trigger powerful emotional responses. The abundance of loss will turn grief into an everyday human experience. Parents will have to explain to their children that animals used to live not just at the zoo but in the wild; that there was a time when rats and squirrels were not the largest animal species found in cities; that our once bio-diverse planet used to bloom with a rich assortment of plants and flowers. That the whole foods we used to eat are now gone, along with the pollinators and the landscapes that are altered and diminished beyond recognition.

At some point, the looming fear of loss has to wake us up — even those fervent climate-change deniers among us who want to keep things the way they are and use a couple weeks of cold weather as proof of the lack of climate change. Grief, if harnessed effectively, could very well guide us through the bottleneck.

TICK TOCK

On my dark days, I wonder if we'll even make it to the end of this century. I worry that scientists will soon predict a point on the calendar at which their data show the bottleneck squeezing us back for once and for all. Like George Orwell's *1984* or Stanley Kubrick's *2001*, a late-21st-century year might very well be recognized as the likely date of our demise. This is not that far-fetched. The Bulletin of Atomic Scientists recently moved their famous Doomsday Clock two minutes forward — to 11:57

Photo: Unsplash / WenPhotos

p.m. — inching us perilously close to that organization's predicted end of humanity.[13] Nuclear proliferation and climate change inaction spurred the clock's adjustment.

I would love for us to prove those atomic scientists wrong.

I'm not a betting man, but I would still lay down odds that we have it in us to make it. That we can evolve and that we will find the love in our hearts and passion for life to change how we see ourselves, each other and our place on the earth. Our innovations, convictions and sheer survival instincts will work in our (and in the planet's) favor. The bottleneck will greatly restrict our options, and huge dark days lie ahead, but I remain hopeful that we'll figure out how to make the necessary massive societal changes to see ourselves through. Besides, what choice do we have? ■

13 www.cnn.com/2015/01/23/us/feat-doomsday-clock-three-minutes-midnight/index.html

THE BOUNDARY OF DISCONNECT

Life, Resilience & a Question of Scale

ORIGINALLY PUBLISHED 2013

Photosynthesis is not particularly "efficient" when viewed through a reductionist lens, but when understood as part of the "whole" of a tree and in turn as part of a whole of a forest, there is nothing so elegant and effective: the process that captures free, abundant, clean energy also builds soil at the end of its useful life.

For the last few years I have been exploring the important relationships between scale, density and sustainability. Scale and carrying capacity–two extremely important subjects — are often completely left out of sustainability discussions, to say nothing of national political debates, when they are in fact integral pieces of the puzzle. Indeed this topic relates directly to social, cultural and economic health, and to environmental well-being.

Our modern societies have completely forgotten the importance of boundaries. We have designed the majority of our societal life support systems using scales that are worse than unhealthy; they have so deeply disconnected us from nature and one another that we are now threatening our own long-term survival on the planet.

Let's look to the lessons that natural systems provide. Nature teaches us how and where to draw the line or boundary around any particular system as ecosystems and even individual species nearly always find the smallest scale within which to operate effectively. Since any action taken by an organism takes energy, nature insists on efficiency because it cannot afford to waste its precious resources. Therefore an organic system typically supports itself by fulfilling its needs within the smallest possible scale, adapting as conditions change. The definition of "the smallest system" may not always be readily transparent however, as there are multiple overlapping conditions that affect the size of a particular boundary, *so a "sweet spot" of nested efficiency* occurs at what may not be the smallest observable scale.

In cases of natural "scale jumping"[1] to a larger than obvious scale, there's usually an efficiency/competitive-advantage from another system that accounts for why a particular boundary is expanded. Perhaps another resource previously beyond reach must be harvested in order to maintain the health of the primary organism? Photosynthesis is not particularly efficient when viewed through a reductionist lens, but when understood as part of the "whole" of a tree and in turn as part of a whole of a forest, there is nothing so elegant and effective: the process that captures free, abundant, clean energy also builds soil at the end of its useful life.

---

1   A concept I coined for the Living Building Challenge

In other words, the scale in which the ant operates is both highly adaptive to multiple interconnected, changeable systems and rigidly applied in the macro context so as to never be overextended, beyond which the colony's resilience and very survival becomes at risk.

I can think of no better creature than the ant to further help illustrate my point. An ant's boundaries are created according to the distance it can safely travel to and from its colony. It must be able to find and carry all of its resources within those geographic limits. Its home is at the center, and all business is conducted outward from that location. It forages for food, seeks information and retrieves the bodies of fallen soldiers always within the established boundary and always returning back to center. When a fallen twig or a rainy puddle stand in the way, the ant takes a detour without losing sight of its original goal, modifying the shape of its territory while remaining true to the larger boundary condition, which is chemically understood by the colony.

That seems like a damn good metaphor for our colonies!

The ant's adaptability reminds us that scales and boundaries are dynamic; healthy boundaries are rarely drawn in perfect circles, and their shapes shift as conditions change. Just as an ant must somehow calculate the pros and cons of navigating around a downed tree in its path—gauging if expending the extra energy is worth the payoff on the other side—we go through similar machinations every day. Is driving farther to the large grocery store worth the extra time and effort, or will the smaller selection at the closer store suffice? Which option makes more ecological, social and economic sense? Which takes less of an emotional and temporal toll? Which will yield greater health benefits to the family being fed? The answers depend on many factors, because there is no one scale that applies to everything. Each system has its own ideal scale and its own appropriate boundary.

This natural process of constant adjustment and subconscious and conscious evaluation is inherent with us as much as with any other species: we are nature! The problem is that, as Homo sapiens, we have gone from a localized species to a globalized species within a timeframe that is completely out of sync with our (or any species) ability to have adapted and internalized the changes. For most of our evolutionary history we have,

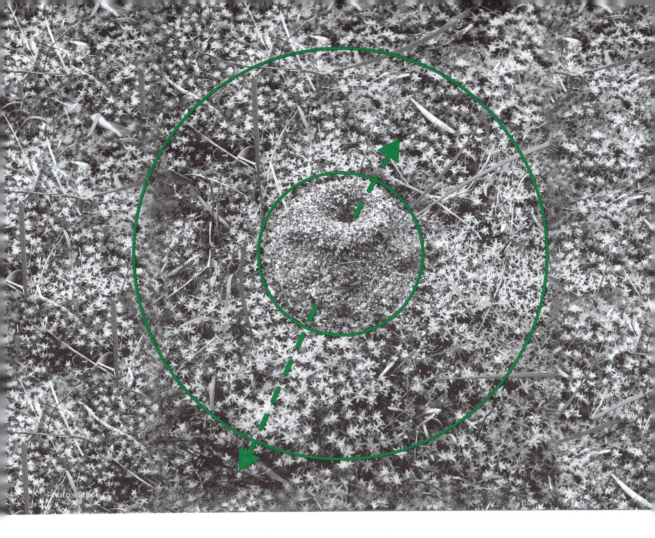

like every other species, lived intensely local lives within a framework of boundaries based on the systems that support us. In the span of only a few centuries[2] (although some of the seeds were sown as much as 10,000 years ago with the rise of agriculture) we have thrown off the perceived yolk of system boundaries and freed ourselves to begin operating outside of the framework of the rest of creation. We are only now beginning to see that such freedom is a reckless technological illusion that will lead to our impoverishment and that the "yoke" of system boundaries was actually a "cradle for life" that sustained us for generations. Imagine that — our boundaries are our cradle!

In many ways our sudden technological and cultural shifts have hidden or obscured the whole notion of boundaries, with the average person completely unaware of where the various things we need to survive come from.

---

2 And if we are realistic about how the average human lives the change is actually only a few decades old.

A REMINDER OF THE SCALE TEST TO DETERMINE BOUNDARY SIZE

By cross-referencing the following scales we can get a sense of the "right" size for any system.

Risk Scale: When the risks of a system's failure exceed those of its benefits, the system crosses the "risk scale barrier." Risks, in other words, must be proportionate to (and in truth should be significantly lower than) the benefits.

Temporal Scale: When the consequences of a system fall to those in a different generation than those who will see the benefits of the situation, it crosses the temporal scale barrier. Risks should be handled by the same generation that benefits from it. Only benefits should accrue through time.

Physical Human Scale: When the size of the system or artifact in question is not relatable to human scale through its design or function and has the effect of diminishing community/human interaction rather than increasing it, it can be said to have exceeded the human scale. Our constructs should create, not diminish, community by bringing us together, not pushing us apart.

Mental Map Scale: When the size of a system cannot be understood, grasped or managed by a small group of people who know and can relate to each other, it has crossed the mental map scale barrier. Decisions should not be made by people who neither understand the consequences of their decisions, nor empathize with those their decisions affect.

Environmental Scale: When the activity of a system permanently degrades the health and biodiversity of any ecosystem, it has crossed the environmental scale. Environmental impacts are inevitable, but working within the functional carrying capacity and natural resilience of a place is essential.

Economic/Social Scale: When a system by its nature only concentrates wealth rather than distributing it, then it has crossed the economic/social scale. When the workers whose labor supports a given system cannot afford to purchase the very things they make, it has crossed this line.

We are only now beginning to see that such freedom is a reckless technological illusion that will lead to our impoverishment and that the "yoke" of system boundaries was actually a "cradle for life" that sustained us for generations.

We have reached beyond what I call the **Boundary of Disconnect**.

- Beyond the Boundary of Disconnect, we become so separate from something that we lose empathy for it or cognitive awareness of the presence of a boundary.

- Beyond the Boundary of Disconnect we lose the ability to even know where the boundaries are or even if there should be boundaries.

- Beyond the Boundary of Disconnect we begin to disrupt other still functioning boundaries since all are interconnected.

- Beyond the Boundary of Disconnect we no longer have the benefit of positive system feedback and we enter a highly un-resilient state. By definition, resilience is broken as this line is crossed.

When any species or its systems operate beyond the Boundary of Disconnect for a sustained period, the overall system of life on the planet eventually self-corrects — colonies collapse, civilizations crumble, species go extinct and a great reshuffling happens. This too is normal and part of the cycle of life. But life gets uncomfortable when the parameters of the ultimate boundary (earth itself) is exceeded.

Our collective illusion, put in place as a result of our technological prowess and propped up by an unusually long period wherein we have operated outside of our own Boundaries of Disconnect, is such that we do not see that the system of self-correction has already begun. In the case of climate change we are seeing some of these system of life self-corrections that we may not be able to reverse or adapt to.

UNDERSTANDING BOUNDARIES FOR TRUE RESILIENCE

The Boundary of Disconnect varies according to the system in question, and even those are constantly changing. Sometimes environmental impacts affect boundaries; other times energy resources dictate changes.

Even psychological factors such as accountability and empathy can redraw the lines for our species.

The point is that we must always be aware of where (at least approximately) the Boundary of Disconnect lies for our various life support systems as we design our cities and our economies. We have fooled ourselves into thinking that the artificial boundaries we've created in the past 100 years are appropriate and sane. They are neither.

It is time to design our community systems that take appropriate scale and boundaries into consideration. Once we factor in the concept of the Boundary of Disconnect, we will have an elegant framework in which to plan all our endeavors. While precise boundaries are impossible to ascertain, it is possible to understand the fuzzy boundaries that do exist.

Let's explore some examples of current systems within our communities that reach beyond the Boundary of Disconnect and that are ripe for radical, more sustainable reinvention:

Water Supply. This one is obvious. All systems for water or waste conveyance should work within knowable watersheds, which are inherently defined by gravity. For this reason, water and waste system should be decentralized, distributed and gravity-based. Given these parameters, it becomes clear that water-related boundaries need to be extremely tight, and water should not be made to flow uphill over miles of terrain. Once water requires pumping from one watershed to another, you have broken the Boundary of Disconnect. It is entirely possible to create a system by which a community becomes completely independent from water outside of its boundaries (even in arid locations) with neighborhood scale water systems.

Energy Supply. As soon as energy comes from a place where its consumers can no longer see or experience its generation and the impacts of the resource extraction that supports it, the Boundary of Disconnect has been crossed. The advent of cheap energy unplugged us from the realities of coal, oil and natural gas production, and we have become disconnected from the sources of the resources we use most hungrily. Ideally, power consumed is matched by energy generated at the site — or at least nearby. It is entirely possible for a city to generate all of its own energy cleanly from within its own boundaries, although currently we transport energy thousands of miles.

Food & Nutrient Systems. We currently treat the entire globe as our snack bar, literally expanding the boundaries for our food systems as far as they can go. Ideally, we should limit the bulk of our food boundaries to within a few hundred miles radius of the community borders, allow-

Water Supply

Seattle gets its water supply from the nearby mountain watershed-primarily by gravity, but many communities get their water from distant aquifers and from many dozens of miles. A healthier paradigm is for each community to work within its own watershed and the annual yearly water "budget" that can be captured by the community without depleting underground aquifers or require vast amounts of pumping energy.

CURRENT PARADIGM

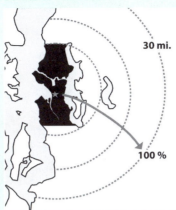

PROPOSED PARADIGM

Energy Supply

Energy in Seattle comes from a few regional sources — some relatively clean and some not so clean. Most communities use energy from highly polluting sources and get that energy from dozens or even hundreds of miles away. A better paradigm is to work within the "current solar income" of a site generating energy renewably and at the source without significant transmission losses.

CURRENT PARADIGM

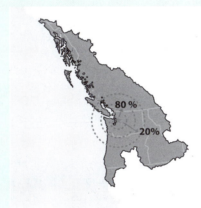

PROPOSED PARADIGM

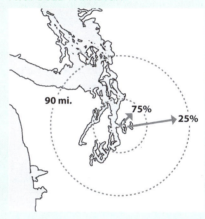

Food & Nutrient Systems

Our food systems in the United States have long crossed the Boundary of Disconnect and the typical calorie travels many thousands of miles. Food should come primarily from local and regional sources — such sourcing creates highly unique regional cuisines

CURRENT PARADIGM

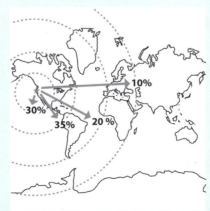

PROPOSED PARADIGM

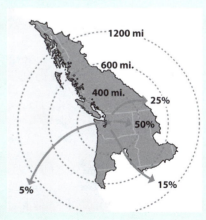

ing only a few exceptions (coffee, for example) to breach those borders. On the opposite end of the spectrum, where currently we destroy the vast quantities of nutrients we consume through conventional waste treatment, instead we should be returning composted nutrients back to the same places that provide us with food; otherwise, we are only degrading soil.

Political Systems. There was a time when political decisions were made by leaders who knew their constituents personally and understood their needs clearly because they shared many of the same localized concerns. Such representation is based on a scale that is small enough for individuals to relate to and with one another — a scale many people believe defines true democracy. Are our giant national boundaries partly to blame for our current trajectory?

Economic Systems. Here, too, there is a limit to how far systems should stretch before they simply break. Once economies extend beyond the Boundary of Disconnect, they diminish in strength and effectiveness. Too small and we lack the capacity for many of the innovations we surely would not want to lose; too large and the consequences become invisible externalities conveniently left behind for the environment and the poor to shoulder. Should we have a global economy for all things? What is the nature of a truly healthy and resilient economy? What scale allows us to have the advantages of technology and specialization without the current global framework that is a race to the bottom socially and environmentally while only a few benefit?

Community Size. Everything from overcrowded classrooms to big-box stores plunked on the edges of towns can be evaluated within this context. It is possible to have too many people in one place, and by extension, too many people for the planet to sustain. Communities must be designed in ways that allow neighbors to relate to neighbors and humans in turn to relate to nature. When buildings climb too high off the ground and suburbs sprawl too far from the social core, our communities have breached the healthy boundary where we are disconnected from each other and from the environment that sustains us. Are cities with over 20 million people, today's mega-cities, inherently a problem?

Material Flows. The supplies we use to build and operate our communities should come primarily from local resources, not be shipped from across the globe. Adhering to the imperatives of the Living Building Challenge's Materials Petal (which limits the physical distance that goods may travel when used to construct a Living Building Challenge project) is one way we are expressing this intent–ensuring that our architecture reflects regional variations while minimizing significant embodied impacts.

Political Systems

It is hard to know the ideal size for any political system, but one thing is certain, direct democracy has its limits and beyond a community scale it is impossible for our leaders to know the majority of their constituents.

CURRENT PARADIGM

PROPOSED PARADIGM

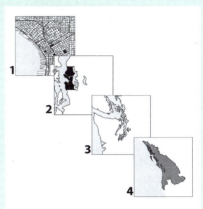

Economic Systems

From an environmental perspective the global economy has been a disaster; goods shipped all over the world wherever labor and environmental regulations are the most lax; people get cheap products but have no exposure to the negative effects of their decisions. Local economies, the world over, become vulnerable to forces they cannot see or control. A healthier economy is one where the majority of what people need are made from within a short geographic distance with only specialty items coming from further afield.

CURRENT PARADIGM

PROPOSED PARADIGM

Once one begins to look at any problem through this lens, logical solutions become easier to identify. When we follow the laws of the natural world, there are clear and obvious limits to what we can and should pursue.

Whether we seek to answer questions related to our built environment or our societal structure, it is always best to evaluate potential answers according to the smallest and most efficient scale possible. Keeping things within sane boundaries keeps us engaged with one another and connected to the world around us. ■

REGENERATING THE WHOLE

From Living Buildings to Building Life

WITH BILL REED
ORIGINALLY PUBLISHED 2013

The premise behind a "Living Future" is that any human activity is an opportunity to engage in a positive and healthy interrelationship with all of life.

Life — the whole of life; that is, every entity and system in a reciprocally beneficial and evolutionary relationship — is the top and bottom line of sustainability.

The governing question about sustaining life for humans revolves around the nature of Homo sapiens' role in evolution. Are we meant to be passive observers? Is our role to conserve what is left of nature? Is it our responsibility to reduce the impact of the damage we cause? Or, are we to be positive and active participants for a thriving future?

The premise behind a "Living Future" is that *any human activity is an opportunity to engage in a positive and healthy interrelationship with all of life.*

The work of life is about focusing on active and conscious participation in the evolutionary process. Specifically, this focus means developing life-supporting relationships and actions grounded in each unique ecological system — the places in which we live or act. This work is the missing half of the practice of sustainable design in the building profession. It is essential, yet insufficient, to minimize or neutralize human impact. From a building professional's point of view, it may seem that delving deeply into interacting with life is an over-reach for the job description. We have worked with more than a few green architects who have made this observation:

I really appreciate the work you are doing in bringing back the health of this ecosystem — land, soil, habitat, community, and the like — but what does that have to do with the design of my building?

The general answer: From the perspective of basic building design, *not much.*

It is clear to an increasing number of green building practitioners that making things more efficient and "less bad" is only one aspect of what is required to be in a sustainable relationship with the living systems on the planet. So, then what is the necessary role and purpose for humans in the profound process of evolution? What is the role of the building professions in leveraging the work of shelter into the world of activating and engaging a conscious and intentional relationship with life? What is required of us and our professional practices in order to become engaged in working with the process of building life as the foundational activity that then informs the nature of the objects such as infrastructure, structured landscapes, and buildings?

Life is viable only through the exchange of energies.

The general answer: A range of premises, perspectives, and skills are part of the new palette of practice called Living System Design. We outline the major elements below:

LIVING SYSTEM DESIGN TRUTHS

Principle One: Only Life Regenerates

It has become very fashionable to talk about regeneration as if our static designs — our buildings and infrastructure — are regenerative. The words, regeneration and regenerative, are being co-opted, which is particularly painful to see since they are such beautiful words.

Buildings should exist only if they allow *life to do what it does*. They either diminish the conditions for life or create a positive framework for engagement and relationships upon which life builds and regenerates. Building design creates the opportunity to engage people and all of life in an ongoing and evolutionary relationship. There are two complementary dimensions to the practice of Regeneration:

- **Regenerative Design** at its entry level is the process for reversing damage and creating the basis for self-renewing resource systems. This dimension is the realm of restoration design practices: restoring the conditions for life to self-organize in ecological sub-systems. Narrowing the purpose of regenerative design only to this level — the threshold work of sustainability — largely ignores the wider and integrated issues relating to the economy, agriculture, education, culture, and so on. Additionally, this narrow scope is often defined within the boundaries of different professional disciplines rather than viewing these disciplines as parts of an integrated system that includes community engagement and stewardship.

- **Regenerative Development** can be characterized as having two interdependent aspects: **1)** a discovery process that determines the right phenomena to work on, or to give form to, in order to inform and provide direction for design solutions that can realize the greatest potential for evolving a system and **2)** a continuous developmental process occurring throughout Discovery, Design, and Post-Construction that builds the capability, the field of commitment, and the caring that encourages stakeholders to step forward as co-designers and ongoing stewards of those solutions.[1]

---

1 Pamela Mang and Bill Reed, *Designing from Place, Building Resource & Information*, 40:1, 23-38

Photo: Unsplash / Jordan Whitt

Regenerative Development is an instrument for achieving true sustainability through re-establishing living systems (socio-ecological-conscious systems) with the capacity to continuously evolve. It develops the capacity in people to become more internally and externally capable. It is not an educational process distinct from the work people are doing; instead, development and work are continuously intertwined with one another.[2]

Principle Two: Life is About Interrelationships

Life is viable only through the exchange of energies. Life increases in resilience and evolutionary potential when water, soil, sunlight, energy, living entities, information, and so on have greater opportunities for exchange.

- Diversity of *relationship* is a minimal requirement for life. For example, a zoo has a diversity of species but does not have a diversity of relationships. Therefore, the potential for a healthy ecosystem is limited.

- To be in a positive relationship with nature means we will best serve it when we are developing the skills to become in positive relationships with other humans and, of course, to have a positive relationship within ourselves. Indifference or violence to nature is unlikely to be successfully addressed until we overcome these same things in our own nature.

2 Pamela Mang, *Regenesis*

Principle Three: Every Place is Unique and Alive and Whole

"Here"... is a whole living entity. Systems nested within inter-related systems; just like the human body.

If we use a human being as an example of a whole system, we might assume that our boundary is our skin. That might be a very dangerous assumption for the continuity of our life. The skin, like the boundaries we assume for all living entities, is a boundary that is not a boundary. If our skin were a solid boundary, we would be dead in an instant. If we took way the larger context of air, water, and food we would die. If we took away the healthy soil and farmers who produce the food; we would die. So, where is the boundary? How do we define it?

Bucky Fuller and a group of students were standing outside and talking about systems. He said: the first thing you have to understand to be able to work with systems is that you have to bound them, and he drew a circle in the dirt with his shoe. The second thing you have to know is that boundary is your creation... it doesn't really exist, and he erased the circle with his shoe. [3]

"There is a distinction between environmental and ecological thinking. By definition, an environment is the context within which something exists. Environment contains an "us" and a "not us" in its meaning. Ecology, by contrast, sees all aspects as part of a working dynamic whole — it's all us." [4]

3   As recounted by one of Bucky's students
4   Carol Sanford, *The Responsible Business*, 2011

Photo: Unsplash / Matthew Smith

- The idea of working with a "whole" system is a bit alien to our culture. A whole is not limited by any boundary. Yet it has a domain or limit within which we might practically act depending on the context. "How big is here?" is a question almost anyone can answer about their community or the place they live. Wholes are more easily qualified by the nature of essential relationships. A watershed is one essential relationship of exchange with which we may have some influence. It may be just a half-mile away or it may be down or up river hundreds of miles. "Here" may be defined by the community and include many watersheds. It comes down to what-affects-us and what-we-affect that must first be defined in order to work with living systems. This systemic relationship is known as a holarchy or nested systems. In general, no living thing is more or less important within this system.[5]

- *It is necessary to look at everything as systems or webs of exchange wherein each element is inextricably tied to all of the others. An element is not separable. It also cannot be included randomly. It matters: Who does it shelter? Who does it feed? What does it store? What exchanges does it enable? At what times? And in what ways? It must relate in many directions, not just to me.*[6]

- A thought experiment may be useful to illustrate the difference between designing an object and developing a whole system of interrelationships.

What is the difference in effect and the nature of design if we simply design a bedroom addition or design a bedroom addition for the purpose of developing the best in our children? In the latter example, where is the effective boundary of the systems our children might be engaged in and influenced by? With each changing thought focus the nature of the design quickly begins to change.

Principle Four: Working with Whole Systems Requires a Pattern Understanding

Because a whole is greater than the sum of its parts, it is, by definition, impossible to understand a whole using a reductionist perspective. This is where working with pattern understanding comes into play. For practitioners familiar with working with patterns, it is actually easier to assess living patterns and reach definitive conclusions from these distinct patterns than it is to try to make sense of thousands of pieces somehow associated — or not — with each other.[7]

We are quite good at this approach when it comes to assessing a whole person: we intuitively know that we will not be able to understand the

---

5 Also reference, Jason McLennan's article "Boundaries of Disconnect," *Trim Tab*, Winter 2013
6 Joel Glanzberg, *Permaculture Mind*, 2013
7 Christopher Alexander's Pattern Language and the Nature of Order series are great resources.

distinct nature (or essence) of a friend if there are only a few organs and bones available for inspection. Even if all of his or her component parts were available, including all the genetic sequencing, it is obvious that the nature of the person could then be described only mechanically, if at all. Yet, with observation, we are able to describe the uniqueness of individuals. We do this by looking at the patterns of how individuals, each as a whole entity, are in relation to other entities — friends, colleagues, family members, their community, a dog in the street, and so on. It is how they are in relationship, what value they add to the relationship, the role they serve and provide that begin to triangulate "who" they are, not just "what" they are. The same holds true for the places we inhabit.[8]

Western and Eastern medicine practices may be a useful comparison.

- Green building, as it is currently practiced in a mechanical manner using LEED or other checklists, can be compared to working on the heart, or intestinal system as a specialist might — curing the particular issue but not addressing the overall systemic nature of the cause, whether it is diet, environment, stress, or genetics.

[8] Bill Reed, *Regenerative Development and Design*, from Charles J. Kibert, *Sustainable Construction*, 3rd Ed, p. 109

Photo: Pixabay / Margarita Morales

It seems an understatement to say that many issues and new perspectives need to be internalized in the development of our capability to live sustainably.

- Integrative Design, an organized process to find synergies among building and living systems, has an analogy in Integrative Medicine — many specialists getting together to diagnose and address relatively complex cause and effects.
- Regenerative Design might be compared to naturopathic and Eastern Medicine — cranial sacral therapy, acupuncture, and so on — as these practices start with the energetic patterns of the whole body.

In practice, all of these practice processes should come into play as they all have value. Yet, it is always better to start with the nature of the larger environmental influences and interrelationships before solving for the symptom and cutting the body open.[9]

Often, practitioners mistake the "flows" of a system as the indicator of relationship. Flows of water, energy, habitat, and sun are certainly important; yet, continuing to use human relationship as an analogue, we would not describe our relationship to a friend only in terms of flows. The aspects of relationship are energetic, often invisible, and full of extremely complex and nuanced exchanges.[10] There is an essence-to-essence relationship occurring, not an element-to-element relationship.

A living system — or place, or watershed, or community — is a "being" or "organism". It has a unique essential nature and therefore has a unique way of expressing itself on an evolutionary trajectory. Thus, it is necessary to be in relationship with it; if we are not, then abuse, neglect, or misunderstood interventions are the result. This nature of relationship is the big leap for the design and building industry. Various aboriginal peoples had this understanding; everything in space and time, including the consciousness of "who" they were was inextricably part of the whole.[11]

The Navajo term for mountain... refers to a whole set of relationships and the ongoing movement inherent in those relationships. These relationships include the life cycles of the animals and plants, which grow at different elevations, the weather patterns affected by the mountain, as well as the human's experience of being with the mountain.

9 Ibid
10 Ibid
11 Ibid

The Challenge is successful because it satisfies our left-brain craving for order and thresholds and our right-brain intuition that the focus needs to be on our relationship and understanding of the whole of life.

All of these processes form the dynamic interrelationship and kinetic processes that regenerate and transform life. Since this motion of the mountain is not separate from the entire cosmic process, one can only really come to know the mountain by learning about the kinetic dynamics of the whole.[12]

All this cautiousness is not to say that working in pieces and parts with quantitative measurement is wrong. It is just not the most productive place to start and never the place to finish. As Wendell Berry observes, *A good solution is good because it is in harmony with those larger patterns... A good solution solves more than one problem and it does not make new problems... health as opposed to almost any cure, coherence of pattern as opposed to almost any solution produced piecemeal or in isolation.*[13] Adopting one or two green or regenerative technologies into a green building practice without understanding the underlying principles that make the approach wholly regenerative are not as effective and, at worst, produce unintended counterproductive consequences.

Principle Five: We are Nature

This standpoint speaks to a positive role for humans in nature. As long as we see ourselves above nature, or worse than nature, we will not be in "right" relationship. A mutually beneficial, or reciprocal, relationship is required of a healthy living system. A forest tree or wetland is not more or less important than a human. We are integral to each other. The role of humanity might best be described as a "gardener", a relationship that is beneficial for the plants, the soil, the watershed, as well as the person.[14]

The design process provides a unique opportunity to explicitly address the potential for humans and nature to be in mutually beneficial relationship.

---

12 Mary Jane Zimmerman, *Being Nature's Mind: Indigenous Ways of Knowing and Planetary Consciousness*

13 Wendell Berry, *The Gift of Good Land*, Chapter 9, Solving for Pattern

14 Good texts to illustrate this point are *1491*, by Charles C. Mann and *Tending the Wild*, by M. Kat Anderson.

SO WHAT?

So what do we do with these Living System Design Truths? For our role in nature to be effective and beneficial we need to address some gaps in our understanding and have appropriate expertise represented on our teams in order to truly practice regenerative design. This expertise must include:

- An understanding of ecological system principles and processes.

- Pattern recognition — or tracking — skills to identify the distinctiveness of the ecologies (including human culture) in the places we are working. For example, patterns point to the roles that places and people play in an ecosystem. (Stories have been the way great civilizations have held meaning and development. Stories hold the complexities and essence of life; they hold, and help us to recognize, patterns.)

- Polymaths with an inherent curiosity in all knowledge and a wide enough span of knowledge to know what they do not know.[15]

- Humility to realize that the project's team very best work will still be open to improvement.

- An expert facilitator and resource to work with the client, the team, and the community in developing a regenerative relationship with "place" and to carry that capability forward into the future — forever.

With this understanding it becomes clear that a new purpose and role for the building industry is emerging. The challenge is to move up the ladder of ecological engagement in order to achieve long-term and positive effect with ALL of life. This repositioning requires movement:

- From techniques and technologies applied in isolated fashion to integrated systems as part of a whole.

- To acknowledge the human role as integral to the health of the whole system of life (inhabiting, not occupying).

- To develop the capacity and capability to continually regenerate a new relationship as life emerges — becoming part of life (co-evolving). This aspect requires the development of a mind that looks towards new potential rather than only solving perceived and existing problems with existing tools.

- Evolution is required to sustain all life (including human life). With this imperative, we need to stay actively involved in evolutionary design, realizing the following:

---

[15] See Jason McLennan's book *Zugunruhe*, Chapter Three about Polymaths.

- Sustainability is not possible without engaging in the process of Regeneration or Conscious Evolution.

- Evolution means to bring something of higher order into being, moving up strata to be able to integrate more complex energies to create greater value (ultimately, there can be no net positive without evolution because of entropy).

We need to understand our purpose as humans and our co-evolutionary role in each unique place we live

This kind of work requires a new way of thinking to shift us from a reductionist worldview. It can not really be adequately described in writing or through dialog because words also tend to fragment us.[16] This work requires experience — it cannot be abstracted like this article, despite our best efforts to convey the issues. It seems an understatement to say that many issues and new perspectives need to be internalized in the development of our capability to live sustainably. It is not simply shifting to a new mental model; it is, as Daniel Pink points out in his book,[17] the development of a Whole New Mind.

ENGENDERING EXPERIENCE — A TOOL TO TRIGGER A MOVE TO REGENERATION

When the Living Building Challenge was launched in 2006 it was done so in a context where the nature of the discussion around sustainability was limited primarily to LEED points and, by definition, a reductionist approach to limiting negative impact. This approach was a natural beginning for the green building movement, as it started at a level that most building practitioners could understand and were willing to engage — start with the way we do things now — and make it a little less bad.

Yet, it was clear that for true and deep success to take place, a new framework was needed as a bridge to the type of holistic, truly regenerative level of practice. It was not enough to have only have a philosophy or to engage only philosophers. After all, Living Buildings had been discussed by Berkebile and McLennan since the mid-nineties and the Regenesis Group in Santa Fe had been pioneering regenerative thinking for at least as long, with minimal uptake. Others, like Sim Van Der Ryn and Pliny Fisk had been advocating ecological design even longer and Buckminster Fuller and Ian McHarg who preceded these individuals, were two of the earliest proponents. Making such a large conceptual jump within practical parameters was and is highly challenging.

---

16 The Tao Te Ching balances this kind of paradox better than any text when talking about the form and the formless.

17 *Drive: The Surprising Truth About What Motivates Us*, Daniel Pink, 2009

The Omega Center for Sustainable Living. Certified under Living Building Challenge 1.3
Copyright Assassi, Courtesy BNIM

A tool that looked just enough like LEED on the surface was required for people to be willing to engage, *but written and codified in such a way that working with it required confronting the very challenges inherent in a reductionist approach.* The Living Building Challenge in many ways is a paradox — a reductionist tool to dismantle reductionist approaches, or as Nadav Malin of Environmental Building News observed, "a manifesto in disguise as a standard."

It was a stealthy way to wean people from one intellectual framework into another. The creation of the Living Building Challenge by McLennan was very deliberate and it has been remarkably successful at getting people from many backgrounds all over the world to begin asking the right questions about our place in the world and what true success with our architecture and communities should look like. It informs us of how to change the standard and associated programs — all the while we are aware that any "tool" created by us or anyone else will always have limitations.

The Challenge is successful because it satisfies our left-brain craving for order and thresholds and our right-brain intuition that the focus needs to be on our relationship and understanding of the whole of life.

The first Living Buildings become living proof that we can go much further than we thought with today's technologies and know-how while shining bright lights on how far even the best Living Building is from our ultimate destination. When truly successful, we will see the light shining right back at us — it is *we* who have needed to change all along! More than seeing a new certified Living Building, we are most encouraged when the program stimulates that electric moment when individuals understand their connection to the whole and the lights go on. It does not happen all the time but it is beginning to happen with increasing frequency.

This is where Regenerative Development comes into practice. As Kathia Laszlo observes, "Sustainability is an inside job." A new way of purposeful relationship and "being" in the world requires a continual process of conscious engagement — a "practice" if you will. Engaging with life in a co-evolutionary (developmental) way requires us to substantially change how we think about life, our role in it, and how we continually engage with evolutionary emergence. This is the "other half" of sustainability.

This article is intended to serve as a bridge between two schools of thought that are now converging in an interesting way. The convergence of improving the efficiency of our technical practices and embracing the effectiveness of working and "becoming" with whole living entities and systems is the ecology we are working towards. The Living Building Challenge symbolizes this convergence. It points the direction towards the verb "living", towards "aliveness."

> **Moving from Living Buildings as a "noun" to that of a "verb" and by putting greater emphasis on regenerative development that can lead to a Living Future is a true convergence of two powerful schools of thought.**

This shift is exciting and full of meaning and potential. This is where Living Buildings converges with the regeneration of a whole living system of mutually supportive interrelationships that is informing the 3.0 version of the Challenge which will be released sometime in 2014.

The living system school of thought represented by Regenesis starts with the understanding (and awe) that healthy living systems have an inherent capacity to continually generate new sources of life for and within themselves and their environment — that is, to re-generate. For human development to be a positive force, the imperative is to enable the system(s) it affects to re-establish its regenerative capacity. The most effective means for doing so is through using the way a project is conceived, designed, constructed, and occupied to create a new living system — one that harmonizes project and place at a new order of regenerative capacity. To develop this capability within humans to engage the necessary and ongoing mutually beneficial relationship with life, the people in that place are challenged to develop the capacity for new understanding and care in order to participate with the ongoing evolutionary processes.

The practice process of regeneration emerged from the work of Charles Krone.[18] It is a school of thinking and being — to see and be one with the working of life as a system of nested and inseparable whole living entities. It takes time and purposeful practice to shift from only seeing the world as separate, machine-like things that are mechanically connected to one another.

The challenge will be to understand that working with aliveness and the development of the consciousness that can hold and evolve with the continual process of emergence is markedly different than working with a mechanical and reductionist worldview. All are necessary and yet require truly different mindsets. Remember that Einstein said, "We can't solve problems by using the same kind of thinking we used when we created them."

Moving from Living Buildings as a "noun" to that of a "verb" and by putting greater emphasis on regenerative development that can lead to a Living Future is a true convergence of two powerful schools of thought. ∎

18 Pamela Mang and Bill Reed, *Designing from Place, Building Resource & Information*, 40:1, 23-38

FALLING IN LOVE WITH LIFE

Our Next Evolution

WITH BILL REED
ORIGINALLY PUBLISHED 2013

What of life can we sustain if we do not love it? And what of life can we sustain if we do not love ourselves?

This article is the second of three. In the first, "Regenerating the Whole, from Living Buildings to Building Life" (published in *Trim Tab* magazine, Spring 2013) we introduced aspects of the *different thinking* required to engage in the practice of living system development or regeneration; how this thinking is different from the left-brain, piecemeal, technical efficiency approach to sustainability; and why this shift is essential to achieve a sustainable condition.

This second piece is intended to emphasize the necessary shift in our *state of being*. This is the right-brain, heart, and consciousness aspect of *human being*. Developing our state of being is not generally considered a useful practice by the culture of Western thought. We demonstrate this bias, or fear, of its legitimacy by limiting our professional focus almost exclusively to the other half of the story. The story the green building community has implicitly been telling is that green techniques and technologies, and the facilitation of human interrelationships, are sufficient. As if, with these efficiencies, we will transform our culture and relationship with life; that somehow, we will be transformed, magically, into understanding and caring for life on the planet in a way that benefits and respects all the living processes and systems. While mechanical technologies must support the effort toward sustainability, the greatest source of leverage is within humanity's inner development and outer practices: developing the understanding of why, and the practice of how, to *be* in right relationship.

The third article will address some processes to *practice living system design and development* and the ways various practitioners are attempting to bridge the world of things and relationships into engaging in the wholeness of life. How do we help our clients, stakeholders, and ourselves live into and develop this way of being?

The role of technology is not to elevate us above nature, but rather to elevate us within our nature, and within nature itself.

THE OTHER HALF OF THE STORY — A CALL FOR GREATER HUMAN-NATURE BONDS

All living organisms are continually evolving as a natural response to ongoing genetic and environmental stimuli. Homo sapiens are also affected and transformed by our ever-changing, omnipresent technology, which affects how we live, what we think is important, what we value, and what we love. Our fascination with, and increasing dependence upon, all forms of technology accelerates our separation from the wonders of the natural world and the interdependent, life-giving processes of all other living organisms. Our technology has, on a personal and experiential level, largely removed us from the natural cycles and seasons of weather and of relationship with other species. Certainly, our awareness of and affinity for the natural world has been altered, just as this disconnect has fueled our disregard for it. As a species, we have exchanged our love of nature for a love of technology and a love of our own cleverness. We have misplaced our love. We need to ask, and answer, a very serious question. What of life can we sustain if we do not love it? And what of life can we sustain if we do not love ourselves?

Advocating for technology as a universal remedy for ecosystem woes is a misguided approach — technology alone cannot save us or our natural environment. The role of technology is not to elevate us above nature, but rather to elevate us within our nature, and within nature itself. As we have witnessed on countless occasions worldwide, technology is a poor substitute for life. From the degradations of land, water and air, from mining and forestry activities to the smog-laden, polluted industrialized cities, we have tried to force our will on nature — but we have suffered the negative consequences. Technology has dulled our sensitivity, our understanding, and therefore our care of the fundamentally essential healthy relationship with how life works and our potential for role in the process of evolution. All that can save us is a sustained awakening of the human heart to nature and the consciousness of our responsibility and role to shift this relationship to one that is mutually beneficial. How do we develop a close and caring bond with nature and, in essence, be one together?

Photo: Unsplash / Havin Rojas

OUR ROLE ON THE PLANET — DEFINING HOMO REGENESIS

In our opinion, the idea of "Homo regenesis" is the next evolution of the human species. Beyond that of a "sapien," or thinking creature, is a creature that thinks, knows, understands, and appreciates its place and therefore the nature — or state of being — of its role in the wider web of life. This evolution will culminate when every human action helps to create greater opportunities for life — rather than diminished opportunities. Although the seeds of Homo regenesis can be found throughout history, especially in a few indigenous cultures, a 'taker' mentality has been preponderant (to use a term from Daniel Quinn in his book *Ishmael*).

The following definition of life resonates with us: "life is the process of becoming,"[1] a continual process of a continual process of consciousness and rebirth. If we aren't evolving, we are dead. And if we are not aware of who we are and how we are being, it is difficult to evolve consciously. So, who are we? What is our position or context within life? What, then, is our role supporting the evolution of all life so that we are supported in return?

1 Author Anaïs Nin, www.brainyquote.com/quotes/quotes/a/anaisnin107685.html

Photo: Unsplash / Mindy Olson P

First, it helps to know that there are patterns of life that can teach us about what it means to be in right relationship with nature. Humans are nature; we are not inherently better than or worse than any other aspect of nature, we are *simply* integral to it. For life to be most diverse, resilient and healthy — meaning whole — humans are supported by, and therefore need to be supportive of, multiple systems of life. Currently we aren't doing so well with this co-evolutionary relationship due to arrogance, ignorance, and a misplaced belief that we are the most important creatures on the planet. In fact, the quality of our lives is nested within smaller universes of living systems and the larger systems that are readily visible, such as forests, rivers, oceans, and other plant and animal habitats.

SYSTEMS OF LIFE SUPPORTING HUMANS

It is helpful to reconceive our place in the natural world — to fully recognize that we are nature. This regenesis requires a new view of ourselves, of our role as a species, and of our relationships within our species and the rest of nature's systems. An important research project is currently bringing some clarity to these intricate interrelationships and offers some valuable insights to how we are not a 'singular species' but part of a beautiful and complex system of life.

> All that can save us is a sustained awakening of the human heart to nature and the consciousness of our responsibility and role to shift this relationship to one that is mutually beneficial.

The Human Microbiome Project (HMP) demonstrates how we should more accurately view our bodies as an entire ecosystem. It brings a new clarity to how complex and connected human life is to other life forms. The scientific evidence on the nature of human life is humbling and makes us see ourselves in a new light. The HMP, under the auspices of the National Institutes of Health (NIH), U.S. Department of Health and Human Services aims to characterize the microbial communities found at several sites on the human body, including nasal passages, oral cavities, skin, gastrointestinal tract, and urogenital tract, and to analyze the roles of these microbes in human health.[2] The NIH notes that traditional microbiology, focused on the study of individual species as isolated units, has not had much success in successfully isolating the majority of microbial species for more in-depth analysis. The researchers suggest that this isolation problem exists because the growth of these species is dependent upon a specific microenvironment that has not yet been replicated in a laboratory experiment.

The human microbiome contains a collective of microorganisms that live both on the surface of and inside the body, in areas such as the mucosal linings, and the respiratory and gastrointestinal tracts. These microorganisms, which consist of bacteria, viruses, and other single-celled organisms, are **estimated to outnumber human cells by a ratio of ten to one and exceed the total number of genes in the human genome by a factor of 200**. While bacteria are often perceived as negative and linked to infections, we are unable to live without them. Our bodies are dependent on bacteria for processes such as digestion, immune regulation, and the production of certain vitamins. In addition to these known and essential functions, the human microbiome may also influence susceptibility to other diseases and chronic conditions like diabetes, obesity, Crohn's disease and Irritable Bowel Syndrome. As a result of its necessary, far-reaching function and its critical significance for life, the human microbiome has even been described as an organ.

To show this critical significance to each of us, consider how a mother's microbiome has a profound, lifelong effect on her children. It is amazing to consider that the only time we exist as a 'singular' species is when we are in the womb — completely helpless and dependent on the mother's health (and that of her microbial community) to live and grow into a

2 commonfund.nih.gov/hmp/index

Only now are we really beginning to learn about and appreciate bacteria as a vital part of our existence, and as just one facet of the entire web of life we rely on — the roles that insects, plants and animals of all kinds play in a mutually supportive fashion.

baby. During birth, as the newborn passes through the birth canal, it is provided with a variety of bacteria that act as a 'starter' for the child's own microbiome and are absolutely necessary for its future life and wellbeing. These microorganisms include bacteria that assist in lactose digestion and help prepare the child for consumption of breast milk. A child born by caesarian section will receive these bacteria from the mother's skin surface but often has a diminished microbiome initially. Breast milk itself performs both prebiotic and probiotic functions, feeding the microbiota and introducing a population of healthful microbes from the mother's intestinal tract.

The point here is that each of us may have only one singular moment as a human self — without bacteria and other microbial cells — when we are a fetus in our mother's womb. Otherwise, we do not exist alone. Our conception of 'self' is skewed and much too egocentric. Only now are we really beginning to learn about and appreciate bacteria as a vital part of our existence, and as just one facet of the entire web of life we rely on — the roles that insects, plants and animals of all kinds play in a mutually supportive fashion.

SCIENCE/TECHNOLOGY CAN STRENGTHEN, NOT WEAKEN OUR CONNECTION TO NATURE

The Human Microbiome Project, with its scientific movement towards a holistic focus on the interconnectedness of the complex whole, serves as a meaningful model for how we should view all human-nature relationships. We can and must use advances in science and technology to provide us with astounding information on, and enhanced understanding of, the nature of life and our connection to life. We are a community and a universe that is constantly changing. We must reflect on what we must become and how we can evolve and then undergo a renewal — a move beyond Homo sapiens... to Homo regenesis.

HUMANS IN SUPPORT OF THE SYSTEMS OF LIFE

Research indicates that past humans had a different relationship with life. For example, before European settlers inhabited the eastern coast of North America, the aboriginal peoples managed the eastern forests in a sophisticated and elegant way by burning 'cold fires' in the spring and autumn, among other techniques. These cold fires consumed the leaf duff from the previous season. They burned quickly and without significant heat, due to the lack of built-up dried and dead material. The fires deacidified and added carbon to the soil, thinned out the thin-barked beeches and maples and allowed the thick-barked chestnut, oak, and hickory trees to thrive. This managed ecosystem allowed for a greater diversity of species and food sources, environmental stability, predictability, and the maintenance of ecotones[3]. The eastern forest had relatively few (but extremely large) trees, which provided openness and protection for multiple levels of food crops. The journals of early European settlers describe these practices and the open nature of the forest that they could drive wagons through — a much different and healthier ecosystem than we have today, even in our park systems.

We now have substantial evidence in support of this. One paper, *References on the American Indian Use of Fire in Ecosystems*, by Gerald W. Williams, Ph.D., of the USDA Forest Service, provides hundreds of sources documenting this way of being.

> **California Indians believe that when humans are gone from an area long enough, they lose the practical knowledge about correct interaction, and the plants and animals retreat spiritually from the earth or hide from humans. When intimate interaction ceases, the continuity of knowledge passed down through generations, is broken, and the land becomes 'wilderness'.**
>
> - *Tending the Wild*, M. Kat Anderson

---

[3] Henry T. Lewis, *Why Indians Burned: Specific Versus General Reasons*, p 77

HOMO REGENESIS RECOGNITION

So, how will we recognize when we are on the correct path to Homo regenesis?

- When we recognize that we are nature
- When we recognize that we are life — we are an ecosystem
- When we recognize we are an important part of an interconnected system and we ourselves are a system
- When we recognize that only life regenerates — not things
- When we recognize that regeneration occurs at all scales, with all life forms
- When we recognize that life requires diversity and diversity is resilience
- When we recognize the uniqueness of all places and fall in love with life
- When we understand our unique role and each unique place we work and live in

> We must reflect on what we must become and how we can evolve and then undergo a renewal — a move beyond Homo sapiens... to Homo regenesis.

In *Tending the Wild*, M. Kat Anderson examines Native American ecological knowledge and the management of California's natural resources prior to the arrival of European settlers. The rich oral history and cultural stories passed on by generations of Native Americans show how these indigenous peoples understood the complexities of living bountifully with, and as part of, the natural system. They were active participants in environmental use, change, and stewardship.

They in fact were gardeners. Gardeners are more than stewards, there is a reciprocal exchange of 'tending' multiple systems of life in a beautiful dance — the soil, the microbes, the plants, the trees, the animals, the human animals. Quite simply, they lived sustainably. Anderson argues passionately that we must make full use of this traditional ecological knowledge, learning from the past, if we are to meet the present-day challenge of thriving.

FALLING IN LOVE WITH NATURE — DEVELOPING A RELATIONSHIP WITH NATURE AND PLACE AS A PROCESS OF DESIGN

Connecting, or reconnecting as the case may be, is the first step in the development of a new or a renewed relationship between humans and the rest of nature — a relationship that leads to understanding, appreciation, liking, and then loving. Analogous to the process that a person typically goes through when falling in love with another person, we need to date and fall in love with nature.

Falling in love is a process. First, we become aware of someone, then we date, then we develop an understanding of that person, and finally we come to love that person for who she or he really is, not simply their first-impression personality or their surface features, **but their essence**.

To carry the analogy further: we may be attracted by certain characteristics of an individual, such as their smile, humor, or intelligence. Yet we also learn to downplay their foibles and negative characteristics, such as anger, impatience, or lack of awareness. Ultimately, what we truly fall in love with is the uniqueness of that person — how the deep and consistent patterns of that person express themselves in interactions and purpose that demonstrate what is really important and meaningful — the core of that being.

Photo: Pixabay / Huskyherz

In a similar way to how we date to find true love of a person, perhaps love of a potential life partner, we have to date nature to find a lifelong love of the natural environment and its true essence. We need to become aware of the strengths and weaknesses of the natural world — specifically the areas near at hand we call home — and gain knowledge, understanding, and appreciation of its complexity by engaging, interacting, and connecting with life in many ways and on many different levels. Only with these personal, engaging experiences can we hope to comprehend nature's complex, yet uncomplicated, living essence patterns and processes, and the interconnection of all life in each unique place. Only then can we develop a love for nature that will be sustained throughout our life. And when we are called into conditions or situations where nature is affected, we can make better and regenerative choices with what we choose to support.

While it certainly is necessary for present-day adults to connect and reconnect with nature, it is critically important that we ensure our children, the future generation of people who must care about and love nature, are introduced and continually connected to all aspects of nature and life. If

Gardeners are more than stewards, there is a reciprocal exchange of 'tending' multiple systems of life in a beautiful dance — the soil, the microbes, the plants, the trees, the animals, the human animals.

we consciously and purposely strengthen the early connection between children and the natural environment, they can learn to love it and then continue this love affair throughout their lives. Simply put, you cannot love what you do not know. It is in their formative years that children are most successfully introduced to, become familiar with, and experience nature in many forms and on many different levels. In effect, this link to nature forms a bonding relationship with life. Children who are encouraged to participate in outdoor activities in natural settings such as forests, streams, lakes, and mountains learn to know and value what nature offers. When they enjoy positive, firsthand experiences like camping, fishing, gardening, and hiking and otherwise get involved with nature, they engage with life on a different and enhanced basis. As a result, they think and act more positively in regard to the natural environment. A love of nature and a love of life are nourished and instilled in their being and will endure over the course of their lives. The dating process with nature has to begin early in children's development. When nature is truly known, it is truly loved. And connecting and reconnecting to life on our planet is a prerequisite and a crucial choice for our own survival.

This process works with adults, too. The opportunity in the process of project design is to develop this understanding amongst the stakeholders. Before design begins, engaging in the understanding of the nature of place and its people can enrich and motivate mutually beneficial relationships. This adds excitement and meaning to the process of design.

FALLING IN LOVE WITH HUMANITY — HUMAN AND COMMUNITY RELATIONSHIPS

We will discuss a few processes to incorporate this way of being and becoming with nature in the third installment of this series. How can we incorporate this process of understanding and create a new relationship in the watersheds and the communities within which we are developing and designing projects? To provide a quick perspective in the interim, we've been using a simple and instructive exercise with various groups. In

It is in their formative years that children are most successfully introduced to, become familiar with, and experience nature in many forms and on many different levels.

this exercise, we ask people to take five minutes to meditate on the nature of the projects and activities they engage in:

In your mind, identify four projects from your experience (a building project, cooking a large dinner with a group of people, a committee working on research — any effort with a beginning, middle, and an end).

Pick two that were successful and two that were agonizingly unsuccessful.

Image the process of working on these projects or activities.

What are the root causes that either limited or created high levels of success?

What made the difference?

Note: Take five minutes to reflect and do not read ahead to see how you'd naturally respond

In the time we've been doing this exercise, we have gotten a huge variety of answers, yet all of the answers share very similar root ideas. In general, success and failure hinged primarily on positive human interactions (motivation, enthusiasm, clarity, intention) and mature personal responses and feelings (trust, humility, lack of ego, empathy). There is always something that is never mentioned as important in these reflections: *Manufactured Technologies & Stuff*. The work of life has first, and most importantly, to do with human interrelationships, the internal ability to manage our own egos, care for each other's ideas and growth, and the larger effect of our work on the world. Successful projects are rarely, if ever, about 'me' or technology.

DEVELOPING OURSELVES AS A PROCESS OF DESIGN

The process of engaging with something larger than us, such as the patterns of life in the workings of nature and our communities, is a humbling and beautiful process. Practicing the process of relationship — a true and mutual learning dialogue around core beliefs, philosophies, and

When nature is truly known, it is truly loved.

purpose — can lead to the founding of common principles for a project. This work of relationship in the context of caring for the different forms of life that comprise the context of a project — the natural and social, the land and city — is the beginning of a profound process of discovery. The key aspect of this work is that it is an intentional practice, not a one-time event or 'charrette.' To be most effective, this transformation requires continual practice — extending long into the future, forever. Relationships, like gardens, must be tended. At a minimum, it seems this work requires a shift in the intention of how we practice the process of design so that we can assist every stakeholder in developing the capability to understand and sustain living relationships. ∎

PRACTICING THE WHOLE

Moving from Ego-systems to Ecosystems

WITH BILL REED
ORIGINALLY PUBLISHED 2016

"You can't work on ecosystems if you are working within an ego-system."

Carol Franklin, Andropogon

In our past articles we introduced aspects of the *different thinking* required to engage in the practice of living system development or regeneration; how this thinking is different from the left-brain, piecemeal, technical efficiency approach to sustainability; and why this shift in thinking is essential to achieve a sustainable condition. Many green projects are generative in nature: people get very excited about the techniques, technologies, and new ways of thinking that result in positive contributions to the health of ecosystems and a reduction of human impact. The big question is how this work can continue in the face of societal inertia and the surprises of evolutionary change. Certainly, a single developer, institution, architect, or planner cannot determine or dictate an effective, long-term result. All living systems of a community and watershed are the only organisms that can influence wholesale, long-lasting and purposeful engagement, and so design should be thought of as a framework or vessel that is supportive of this engagement.

The first article focused on Living System Design Truths, emphasizing five principles inextricably connected to living system regenerative design and development. The second article emphasized the necessary shift in our *state of being*—the right-brain, heart, and consciousness aspect of *human being*. The greatest source of leverage for this needed shift is within a human being's inner development: developing the understanding of why, and the practice of how, to be in the right relationship with the world and each other.

This article addresses some processes to *practice living system design and development* and ways to bridge the world of things and relationships into re-engaging in the wholeness of life. The *re* (which means to do again, afresh, anew) in *regenerative* is the ultimate focus. How do we build the desire, the capacity, and the capability of a group of people to continually engage in a process of rebirthing their relationship with the evolutionary processes of life so that, overall, all life benefits? What does practicing regeneration look like? What are the leverage points that can serve as entry points to practice this way of doing and being?

BROAD ASPECTS OF THE PRACTICE

Regenerative development and design is a living systems approach to design and construction processes, inviting us to consider our full potential as human beings, understanding that we can be in a co-creative role within nature, helping to nourish and be nourished by all of life.

Holding the complexity of the whole of living entities (a person, the land, a community, an organization) is accomplished by working from the core identity (essence or uniqueness) of that entity. Carol Sanford, an expert in regenerative business, describes this as "working essence to essence". "This is a design process that engages and focuses on the evolution of the whole of the system of which we are part. Logically, our place—community, watershed, and bio-region—is the sphere in which we can participate. By engaging all the key stakeholders and processes of the place—humans, other biotic systems, earth systems, and the consciousness that connects them—the design process builds the capability of people and the 'more than human' participants to engage in continuous and healthy co-evolutionary relationship."[1]

Much like yoga, or any body-and-mind practice, a regenerative approach works at multiple levels in the individual and in the collaborative space.

---

1 7group and Bill Reed, *The Integrative Design Guide to Green Building*, pg 45

Photo: Pixabay / janeb13

And it works much like a developing relationship between two people or a group. It is not a mechanistic or "cookie cutter" methodology. The practice responds to what is real and live in the here and now, not through reading words and manuals, but through action and experience. So, as a way of working, a regenerative approach calls for the kind of reciprocity and engagement between the participants, other people and the living system of a place. It is an ongoing tending, aligning, developing, and deepening of relationships—to bring the (birth, life, death, rebirth) process alive in a meaningful and fiercely pragmatic way that benefits life in each unique place.[2]

Regeneration is a practice; it is ongoing, just as evolution is ongoing. It is real work.

Just like life, one cannot go on autopilot and expect to accomplish much of anything. To be most effective in life, with every step we take, we must be conscious of taking the next step.

ASPECTS AND DISTINCTION OF THIS DEVELOPMENTAL SYSTEMS PRACTICE

Regenerative design is not a cookie-cutter, step-by-step, or linear process. As in any holistic practice, it is important to simply begin, and then you are in a position to practice and learn. This may seem to be an intimidating way of launching into this work, yet there are several schools of thought and practice to support the learning curve and help the practitioner engage in the process of socio-ecologic development along with the development of their own lives. For example, the two of us belong to different yet synergistic schools of thought relative to regenerative design. Working with actual projects in this way is one of the most effective ways to engage in large-scale transformation processes toward deeply sustainable, resilient, and regenerative systems.

There are many ways to structure whole, regenerative or integral practices. The important point of this work is to shift your client's approach and assumptions as well as your own (even if you think you have all the right answers) and to start from what is core to the life of that client and to the place and culture in which you are working. This is the shift from doing things to developing the being relationships discussed in the second article. This discovery process of relatedness—between each other, and the whole living organism of the place we are addressing—is the source of compassion and care and therefore of the will to create tremendous change.

---

2 Conversation with Caroline Robinson of Cabal in New Zealand.

From practical experience, we have found that there are some basic aspects and distinctions that are useful to shift a project into this "becoming state." This state of being generates the will to significantly change the way we do things. A master plan, building, or project emerges as a synchronous outcome of these deeper relationships.

These aspects and distinctions can be loosely identified as the **Five Ps of Regenerative Development**:

I. **POTENTIAL:** Co-discovering the new relationships, adaptation, and harmonization possible as people and place evolve.

   Permission: Getting buy-in and endorsement from those involved to begin a different kind of process.

II. **PROCESS:** Building a web of relationships using Integrative Design, Lean Construction or similar processes.

   Five Capitals and Value-Adding Processes: Integrating continuously accruing value into a place.

III. **PLACE AND PEOPLE:** Place and people are linked in a dance — understand what makes this dance unique, its essence.

   Pattern: The consistent and repeating way a living system adds value to itself and other systems.

   Purpose and Role: Understanding and becoming aligned around the unique role people have within this ecology and the role of this place in its larger ecological context.

IV. **PERSONAL DEVELOPMENT:** Practicing and developing a self that can minimize attachment.

V. **PERPETUAL CAPABILITY BUILDING:** Developing whole-systems understanding, participating in feedback systems and opportunities for improvement and discovery as a living process over time.

Important Note: These aspects and distinctions are experienced as concurrent and parallel threads. They are woven together in a way that is most appropriate for each project and the client's level of focus and understanding as a foundation for the physical realization of the project.

In other words, these aspects of the work of engaging a whole living system are all done at the beginning of the project and are deepened and iterated throughout. A continual birth, life, death, and rebirth occurs in the project and within the team and each individual at almost every step of the project when working this way.

Photo: Unsplash / Jesse Bowser

POTENTIAL: NATURE DOESN'T HAVE PROBLEMS; IT ONLY HAS POTENTIAL.

Even seemingly cataclysmic events are not problems. Nature can only address the present and work toward a future wherein life in that place organizes and collaborates to bring a higher order of diversity and resilience. It is a human perspective that looks at these events as problems; instead, it is more fruitful to think of them as rebirths. For example, a stream is in a continual process of making itself.

Since humans are nature, this means there is a lot to look forward to: the most exciting, powerful, and effective dimension of the practice of regeneration centers on working with the concept of potential; that is, *the inherent ability or capacity for growth, development, or coming into being.*[3]

The idea of potential may seem to be stating the obvious: life is emergent, it is becoming, it is always evolving; we are part of an inevitable dynamic process. Yet, in general, our design culture has been trained to solve problems and provide "deliverables"—things, master plans, re-

[3] dictionary.reference.com/browse/potential, October 31, 2015.

Photo: Pixabay / SCY

stored ecosystems, and reports—as if the thinking and ideas delivered at the end of a contract will somehow outlast the myriad evolutionary pressures of life. We can easily lose sight of the whole in pursuit of the part.

What is most fun and satisfying about the practice of regeneration is that we are helping people experience and become excited about the processes of life and how any ecological system—all of life, humans and "nature"—can continually organize to bring back a tremendous diversity of healthy relationships and further the ongoing renewing of quality of life. This regeneration includes our own relationship to self.

This work is built on the concept of autopoiesis,[4] or auto-creation, wherein living beings such as bacteria, guilds of animals, plants, and soil, watersheds, and so on are seen as systems that produce themselves in a ceaseless way. Similarly, we need to take the abilities of the organisms we call human beings, help them see the potential of how life wants to work in the places they live, and then give them basic **organizational frameworks and principles** for how the whole socio-ecological system can be collaborative and healing. With the catalyzing of this co-creative process, whole ecosystems can begin organizing toward a dynamic resiliency in a matter of months and certainly within only a very few years.

---

4   This word appeared for the first time in the international literature in 1974, in an article published by Varela, Maturana, and Uribe, en.wikipedia.org/wiki/Autopoiesis, November 1, 2015.

Nature can only address the present and work toward a future wherein life in that place organizes and collaborates to bring a higher order of diversity and resilience.

Permission: Finding the client who is ready to engage in exploring potential—to move beyond expected outcomes

From residential construction to whole cities and cultural groups within nations, the size of the project doesn't matter. It is important to identify the client's motivating factors in order to deepen the regenerative design process. In our experience, there are a few reasons that clients are inspired to engage in this different nature of design process:

- A desire to leave a legacy compared to their previous work;
- An aspiration toward higher levels of sustainability and restoration;
- Need to address large-scale, human-caused ecological system damage;
- Fear of community backlash and lack of support;
- An awareness of the benefits of systems thinking and integrative processes;
- Collaboration and alignment with multi-stakeholder constituencies and/or large design teams;
- A desire to add value to the system they are working within;
- A desire to systematically address multiple and concurrent issues.

Despite the client's motivation, the general approach to the regenerative design and development process is intended to help them recognize and understand the core of their reason for considering engaging a practice that explores new thinking. The basic way of starting a co-creative relationship is to help clients see themselves and recognize the (likely unspoken) core purpose for their work. This occurs through asking them gently destabilizing questions for which you (and them) do not have an immediate answer. These questions may be entered on identifying the client's distinct purpose for doing this work. The important point to remember is that this is all about them, not about your expertise. One thing is certain: you cannot force this way of being on a client; it is something they recognize when they engage with it.

PROCESS: BUILDING A WEB OF RELATIONSHIPS

At its most basic level, practicing regenerative development is about the process of inviting and helping the stakeholders in an ecological system to be in a continually enriching relationship around a unifying purpose. People, in general, are social beings who want to be in healthy relationships with each other. Fragmented issues and groups of people working in silos and managing their own fiefdoms will only exacerbate the problems in a living system. The most practical and well-developed practice modes come from the world of System Integration. Your "gateway practice" may be built on one of a number of different modalities of group process alignment: community organizing techniques, organizational development, lean construction, integrative process, integrated project delivery. Each of these management technologies has strengths and weaknesses. The most important attribute to be embraced is the idea of organizing around a co-creative or integrated process and avoiding the command-and-control mentality that sponsors the tyranny of the expert. The **integrative process** is an absolute and basic foundation to realize regenerative development. A core group of people in an organization or community must be able to contribute to a process of creativity

Photo: Unsplash / Robin Yang

> *"A diverse community is a resilient community, capable of adapting to changing situations. However, diversity is a strategic advantage only if there is a truly vibrant community, sustained by a web of relationships. If the community is fragmented into isolated groups and individuals, diversity can easily become a source of prejudice and friction. But if the community is aware of the interdependence of all its members, diversity will enrich all the relationships and thus enrich the community as a whole, as well as each individual member. In such a community information and ideas flow freely through the entire network, and the diversity of interpretations and learning styles—even the diversity of mistakes—will enrich the entire community."*
>
> - Maturana and Varela (1987) *The Tree of Knowledge*, as cited in: Fritjof Capra (1996) *The Web of Life*. p. 330

in order for them to eventually take responsibility for the health-giving evolution of the place. If the team that the core group is working with is not integrated there is not much hope or practicality in thinking that a bad example will somehow inspire the opposite.

A unified team is much more intelligent and effective than any individual.

Five Capitals and Value-Adding Processes: Building a web of relationships also means we are building capital, or adding value, to the system in all the essential domains of life. The Forum for the Future, an independent non-profit organization specializing in solutions for sustainability challenges, identifies at least five domains that require value to be added on a continuous basis: Natural Systems, Human Development (spiritual/intellectual), Social Development, Economic Development, and Built Environment. Engaging with, and developing all, five capitals as the design process progresses is why it is vital to "design the design process." If we do not intentionally hold multiple places in the schedule to continually iterate around these domains many opportunities for synergy will be lost.

"…The future is not just about firefighting and tinkering with the surface of structural change. It's not just about replacing one mindset that no longer serves us with another… It's a future that requires us to tap into a deeper level of humanity, of who we really are and who we want to be as a society. It is a future that we can sense, feel, and actualize by shifting the inner place from which we operate…

This inner shift… is at the core of all deep leadership work today. It's a shift that requires us to expand our thinking from the head to the heart. It is a shift from an ego-system awareness that cares about the well-being of oneself to an eco-system awareness that cares about the well-being of all, including oneself… When operating with eco-system awareness we are driven by concerns and intentions of our emerging and essential self – that is, by a concern that is informed by the well-being of the whole."

- *Leading from the Emerging Future*, Otto Scharmer, Katrina Kaufer, 2013

PLACE AND PEOPLE: EXPAND THE OPPORTUNITY IN ORDER TO UNDERSTAND THE ECOSYSTEM AT ITS CORE

In other words, the core living patterns of place and people are observable in their larger context.

We cannot reduce a problem to the point at which it can no longer stay alive. Once a problem is disassociated from its living and supportive context, it cannot sustain itself. Thus, we need to enlarge the system with which we are working:

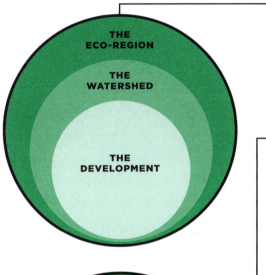

Place: "Place" is the smallest unit of effective living development.

A living system self organizes most effectively when it comprehensively encompasses as many aspects of evolving life as possible: a watershed, agricultural land, relatively undamaged habitat, and urban and rural human habitation.

People: Interestingly, this work also expands into the inner human dimension of self—our own evolving development.

Regeneration is foremost a developmental practice, a process of internal becoming, a process of relationship-building between people-to-people and people-to-nature. The "deliverable" of a project emerges out of this new and deeper exploration and understanding of necessary interrelationship, the unique relationships between the people and the environment, and the unique ecosystem in each place.

"An object seen in isolation from the whole is not the real thing."
- Masanobu Fukuoka, *The One Straw Revolution*

"Start with universe."
- Buckminster Fuller

"If you can't solve a problem, enlarge it."
- Dwight Eisenhower

JASON F. MCLENNAN

Photo: NASA

PATTERN – STORY OF PLACE®

Patterning is how we hold any complex idea. It identifies the consistent and repeating way a living system or living entity adds value to itself and to other systems and entities.

"The world around us can be understood as structures, or as patterns. We can see objects or we can see the exchanges between those beings. Both are valid and useful views, but as a culture, we tend to the myopic view of a formal world. We are highly literate in the languages of symbols like letters, numbers, codes, and icons, and largely illiterate in the language of patterns. Life is process, and processes are patterned. This shortsightedness is why we damage the living world and cannot seem to stop it. We stumble without the balancing view of the pattern perspective."[5]

> "When the uniqueness of a place sings to us like a melody, then we will know, at last, what it means to be at home."
>
> - Paul Gruchow

This pattern work is done through a process of working from pattern understanding to identify key leverage points:

5 Joel Glanzberg, *Pattern Mind*, p.3

"We are looking for what Gregory Bateson called 'the difference that makes a difference.' That difference is not a thing: it is a place and time—a relationship—a small change that changes everything. To play a song well, tune your instrument . . . To topple the arch, remove the keystone . . . Bread rises from adding a timely pinch of leaven… It is not a new technique or technology that is called for, but understanding when and where efforts can be effective . . . To be effective, shift the underlying patterns. This is the key to systemic change… The trick lies in seeing it."[6]

The Story of Place® is a process developed by the Regenesis Group to engage communities in an essence understanding of how the core patterns of life work in the system they live within. Understanding the essence of the place inspires people to work with the system by harmonizing their actions with its core nature. This process builds 'will' in people by helping them relate to, understand, and love the unique way life works in their place. The Story of Place® is not just a narrative of history; it is a narrative that identifies the key nodes of exchange and transformation and the collection of patterns that make a place unique, as all places are. The story is really about the essence of the place and its people. The power of working with a community comes when people are asked to think into the patterns that are being discovered. When they feel the resonance (that "sings to us like a melody"), you know that their heart is being spoken to. Now, the reconciling work can begin between people and the place they know as home.

The International Living Future Institute began pioneering some work to create both "child-centered patterns" and ecological patterns that are based loosely on Christopher Alexander's *Pattern Language*.

PURPOSE AND ROLE: UNDERSTANDING AND BECOMING ALIGNED AROUND THE UNIQUE ROLE PEOPLE HAVE WITHIN THIS ECOLOGY

When exploring a working relationship with a client or consultant, it is useful to shift the conversation from the normal telling and teaching to helping them experience the additional dimensions that need to be considered when working with living socio-ecological systems. By participating and experiencing the work required to move the conversation beyond the normal "what we are going to do for you" or what is wanted, new insights emerge, and the participants are excited about new areas of discovery.

Typically we work with *what* we are going to do. This is the checklist approach. When we add the dimension of *how* it is going to be done, and

6 Joel Glanzberg, *Pattern Mind*

what the purpose is, the conversation and learning are more relevant at a deeper level.

One framework that is used to explore and experience these additional dimensions is the Five Whys. Edwards Deming[7] used this problem-solving tool in his work with the Japanese automobile industry. Any decision made should be questioned to at least five levels of why. This framework demands that we examine levels of understanding and relationships.

"What," "How" and "Why" are the questions all journalists are expected to address to create a whole story.

Harmonize, don't compromise.

Patterning, the Story of Place®, essence understanding, and identifying purpose are ways that help us to get to the core of the issues. This is a kind of tracking process. Trackers are expert at recognizing related and repeated essential patterns at different scales. This kind of training helps us move past all the extraneous white noise and get at what is truly important and repeated over time. By getting to the core, we then have the flexibility to move beyond fragmented wishes and expectations. This is a very effective way to discover new potential.

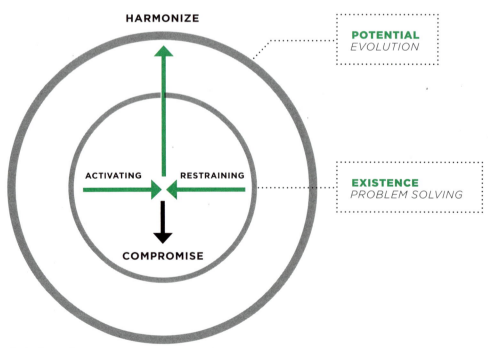

7 deming.org/

> "Practicing personal leadership begins with the 'self' rather than the 'other.'"
>
> - *Personal Leadership*, Schaetti, Ramsey, Watanabe, pg. 14

All life can be seen as an activating force and a receiving or restraining force. For example, a developer wants to build a building, and the receiving force may be the reduced health of the social and natural systems of a community and its habitat. If we compromise, the building may cost a little more, but the local system of nature may still be damaged with a mechanical approach to the problem. By taking the time to find out what is core to the developer and core to the community, we can find multiple ways to identify new potential rather than compromise around what we think we need or the answers we have used in the past.

PERSONAL DEVELOPMENT

How do we develop caring relationships with others in our organizations, communities, and of course, with our inner selves? This work is holistic, and the practice of regeneration asks us to engage ourselves, our clients, and the communities we are involved with in the challenging work of human development in order to effectively work with the collaborative nature of nature.

When we work this way with any group of people, the way of being and becoming will naturally unfold as we challenge ourselves to think in new ways with the places we inhabit. The discipline of sustainable design requires this of us. This is why the term regenerative development is used: as long as life evolves, we will need to evolve with it. This is a conscious process, and working on projects with a diversity of people is one of the best ways to develop new capacity and capability as individuals. It is up to each of us to find a way to intentionally bring this practice into the projects we are working within. Doing so will allow us to be inspiring and powerfully effective with those who hunger for greater meaning in the work of sustaining life.

> "Let him who would move the world first move himself."
>
> - Socrates

"External regeneration cannot occur without internal regeneration. Find a way, or an ecology of ways, to heal your inner self. This could include traditional therapy,

peer-to-peer counseling, group work, or a commitment to one of the many schools of human potential and personal development. A spiritual practice can be included, but is not enough to fully heal the wounds that each person carries from the current oppressive society."[8]

Perpetual Capability Building: Sustaining ourselves and the living systems that support us is a dance of reciprocity, very much like a permaculture food system, or how a gardener engages with her backyard vegetable patch. This attitude and relationship are built upon in order to "garden" the whole system that we live within, and the attitude and practice expand to all living entities.

Regeneration is about engaging in a process of continual adjustment and change based on how natural systems are responding—as well as engaging our willingness to change and adapt by consciously working on our individual selves and the larger social system.

The ultimate deliverable for a regenerative development project is to leave the place, the community, and the ecosystem with a core group of people who have the capability to continue evolving this developmental process into the future, in order to ensure that the project lives into its potential.

This core team may be a newly formed group representing the various domains or interest areas that form the subsystems (energy, water, mobility, social, governance, and so on) that are part of the whole system. The purpose of this team is to "hold the whole," bringing together or informing others who are working in the subsystems so that they are working in support of the unique nature of that particular place.

Based on change and transformation experience (and common sense), this core team will typically need some guidance and support over a period of three to seven years. It takes that long to develop new patterns of relationship that have staying power. This does not take extensive time; it is a matter of consistency, with coaching visits every six to eight weeks to keep the plates spinning and the depth of understanding developing. In other situations, we have seen the process of feedback systems actually teach the community about right relationships. If you have stormwater runoff pollutants draining into the lake your children swim in, the motivation and constant awareness of cause and effect are obvious and compelling.

---

8 "Regenerative Enterprise," Roland and Landua

Finally: *Regeneration* is another term for rebirth in all its dimensions. After all, a whole is composed of everything. Regeneration can start with anyone hoping to make a change for good in the world. Whether we are engaging with a human, a building, a stream, or a whole ecosystem, the relationships are equally complex and always evolving. No matter where we begin, it always comes down to human development; humans are both the source of degradation and the conduit for the greatest expressions of love and co-creation.

One final word on this work as a practice comes from Wahiduddin, a website with a variety of resources for inner exploration and inspiration. ■

> "...simply reading the words are not the point... The goal here is mastery. It is the act of practicing these ideals in every moment of daily life (that) is the challenge, and for most of us that takes repetition and effort, day after day, year after year."
>
> - wahiduddin.net/saki/saki_origins.htm

NESTED TIME ON THE BRAIN'S RIGHT SIDE

Holistic Thinking, Time Management & Making Risotto

FROM *ZUGUNRUHE: THE INNER MIGRATION TO PROFOUND ENVIRONMENTAL CHANGE*
ORIGINALLY PUBLISHED 2010

"They say I'm old-fashioned, and live in the past, but sometimes I think progress progresses too fast!"

Dr. Seuss

It is human nature for us to tackle challenges by first attempting to define the problem at hand within the context of our previous experiences and existing knowledge. We can not help it; that is all we know, so that is all the information we have with which to deal with new situations. The obvious problem with this approach, however, is that it limits us to a set of possible answers that may not be suitable for the questions we need to ask. We end up working within a construct that defines us — and imprisons us.

When we seek to make real change in our lives and in our businesses, we must begin by thinking beyond the limits of our own experiences, and by turning our own conventional thinking on its head. But how do we do this?

DRAWING ON THE RIGHT SIDE

In 1979, an art teacher named Betty Edwards published a groundbreaking book called Drawing on the Right Side of the Brain after conducting research on the ways in which both hemispheres of the brain contribute to, as well as hinder, learning. In the book, she demonstrates the powerful truth that the left side of our brain, which is devoted to logical and analytical thinking, actually hinders our ability to learn to draw and visualize precisely because it "thinks" it knows how to solve the problem of drawing when in fact it does not. Most people experience frustration upon attempting to draw and very few pursue it further than what elementary school requires. When one says," I can't draw," it is actually the left brain that can not draw. Edwards' techniques have shown thousands of people how to "shut off" their left brains and learn with their right brains, allowing even those with no apparent artistic talent to make dramatic leaps in creative performance in short periods of time. Techniques include drawing upside-down and obscuring elements of a picture so that the left brain does not try to "finish" an effort based on what it "knows." Edwards shows what is possible when we take ourselves out of the paradigm to which we have become accustomed — only then are we able to recognize the changes that need to take place. This observation is not to say that right brain dominant people get it and left brain people do not — not at all. We have all seen incredibly creative people unable to function and solve simple problems because they have not known when to change the way they think. We have two sides of our brain for a reason. It is time that we use both of them.

THE TIME OF YOUR LIFE — AN EXAMPLE

Time is a human-made construct that governs and restricts us. It has the power to become our greatest limiter, our biggest source of personal frustration and the greatest barrier between us and our ability to create profound change. From the time we are little, we are taught to think of time in a purely linear fashion. Like so many things in our lives, one thing happens after another, end of story, and we do not challenge it. When we look at time management from a new angle however, we give ourselves the power to drive major change in our own lives.

It is cliché to say that time is precious. Anything finite and limited is such. Add the increasing pace with which we insist on living and the countless tools that help us squeeze more into our days and it is no wonder everybody feels pinched. Time is a valuable commodity, yet how many of us really look at how we spend it? Do we do all we can to get the most out of the time we have? Is there a connection between the way we spend time and the quality of our lives and our happiness? And here is a big one: is there a significant environmental impact when we mismanage or lose track of our time? Let us take a look at a couple of reasons why we are so short on time.

REASON ONE — TEMPORAL PARASITICS

Most of us do not really understand where our time goes during any given day. To paraphrase my good friend Ron Perkins,[1] "You do not know what you do not measure, and what you do not measure you do not really understand." A big problem for most Americans is a phenomenon that I call temporal parasitics.

Parasitics is an energy efficiency term used to describe equipment that draws power even when not in use. Nearly every household appliance is a parasitic load once plugged in. A conventional television set, for example, draws electricity when plugged in, even while off, which costs its owners money and creates pollution. The primary justification for this particular parasitic is to keep the set's internal tube warm so that the picture appears as soon as the TV is turned on rather than taking several seconds to heat up. This momentary convenience — this brief time-saving advantage — drains energy all day and all night, year-round. Is instant gratification worth the pollution that is generated and money that is wasted to achieve it? The notion of holistic time management asks the same question.

---

[1] Ron Perkins is the CEO of a consulting firm called SuperSymmetry USA and is one of the most innovative engineers on the continent.

> For many Americans, the decision to buy into the "American dream" has been disastrous — for their families as well as the environment — as it is often driven more by a desire for possessions and status than by genuine need.

In life, there are a million little things that we do each and every day in order to maintain our lifestyles. Our small decisions support our big ones regarding where we live, what we do to support ourselves and how we define success. We ignore these seemingly insignificant decisions because we consider them trivial; we think of them as unnecessary and we do not take them into account when we make important choices. But I believe we should make them visible because, in sum, they account for the vast majority of our wasted time. They suck away time; they are temporal parasitics.

Any major life decision comes complete with a whole package of hidden temporal parasitics that are either small or large, depending on the course of action. Whatever their magnitude, they have serious implications. One need only look at the number of Americans whose financial liabilities hurl them into endless cycles of work and debt reduction to see how temporal parasitics have the capacity to ruin health, happiness and home life. For when you are in debt, you are not in complete control of your time.

For many Americans, the decision to buy into the "American dream" has been disastrous — for their families as well as the environment — as it is often driven more by a desire for possessions and status than by genuine need. The typical dream scenario involves buying a large house in the suburbs, at least twice as big as the house the buyers grew up in (and now serving a smaller family) instead of living closer to work in a more integrated, multi-use neighborhood. This decision has led the average American to spend a significant amount of time and money each day commuting to work (and generating more emissions) and running errands made necessary by the great distances between services. Even more time is spent maintaining the oversized homes and hiring help to clean it, which of course requires more work hours to fund.

Other examples roll in:

- We accept jobs that require overtime or indirect work-related time in order to generate more income to pay for the mortgages on the big houses.
- We purchase additional vehicles to shuttle us to and from our jobs, often spending additional time looking for parking or being stuck in rush-hour traffic.

Temporal dilution refers to activities that we do not need to do, and many times do not even particularly want to do, yet we do out of habit, boredom or stress. They do not add value to our lives, but we seek them out nonetheless.

- We invest in elaborate wardrobes to support our professional positions and because of a lack of time spend more time and money on dry cleaning and laundering.

- We spend more time eating out since we do not have time to cook at home.

And the time-eating cancer grows...

Like their energy counterparts, temporal parasitics usually impose an environmental burden as well. For each mile it crawls through traffic, the average automobile produces between .5 to 1.5 pounds of carbon dioxide, which also contributes to the creation of ground level ozone, particulates and other threats to our health. Eating "convenience" food — including pre-packaged meals and menu items from fast food restaurants — is as bad for our health as it is for the environment, given the energy and resources used to package, process and ship the food as well as the industrialized agricultural systems needed to support it.

REASON TWO — TEMPORAL DILUTION

Temporal dilution refers to activities that we do not need to do, and many times do not even particularly want to do, yet we do out of habit, boredom or stress. They do not add value to our lives, but we seek them out nonetheless. For many people, watching television is a great example. Certainly there can be quite valuable programming, but too many Americans and Canadians use television like junk-food, endlessly flipping channels and not digesting anything meaningful or intellectually nutritious. I call it temporal dilution because it typically refers to activities that we do not notice or account for but, bit-by-bit, siphon time away from more meaningful things. Many of our unproductive or unfulfilling activities occur just a little bit at a time, and therefore we do not experience their cumulative effects consciously. We are not aware in the moment how much time we spend — or waste, depending on your perspective — engaging in these activities. We do know, however, that we always feel the time crunch and there never seems to be enough hours in the day to do all that we want and need to do. Time dilution makes it difficult for us to see the incentive to change. We justify enormous hours away: "What does it matter if I watch an hour of television every day or commute for forty-five minutes to my job? That is not much time, and many people watch much more television than I do and have much longer commutes." But here is the rub: rationalizations such as these prevent us from devoting our time and living our lives the way we would like to — and being effective in the coming years ahead will require us to be much more consciously in control of our time.

With time dilution, we do not notice things even though their cumulative effects are just as damaging to our health and well-being as if they happened all at once.

Let us begin to think on "the right side of our brain" and take a closer look at how we spend our time.

What if we had to lump together all the time we spend in, say, a year on each time-diluting activity, and examine how our twelve month schedule would map out? I believe that such an exercise would make us all learn a few things about the priorities that we set and how to get on the path to becoming green warriors.

The typical American working adult has the following habits:[2]

- Sleeps an average of 7.5 hours each day
- Works 8 hours per day
- Spends 1.2 hours commuting to and from work
- Spends 1.1 hours daily eating and drinking (although increasingly while commuting to and from work)
- Devotes 2.6 hours to leisure and sports every day
- Spends 1 hour a day in the bathroom (doing all sorts of things)
- Watches 3.5 hours of TV each day
- Cares for others for 1.2 hours each day
- Engages in other household activities for 1 hour each day
- Spends the remaining time in miscellaneous activities[3]

---

2 These statistics are averages based on a variety of sources. Readers are encouraged to insert their own hours to get a sense of how it may work for them.

3 In case you are wondering why this does not add up to 24 hours, keep in mind that these are all averages from various sources and not from a real person. Each person's mix, based on current understanding of time and physics, would add up to 24 hours. There may also be some "double-counting" as people do tend to do multiple activities at once, such as eating while watching TV.

Photo: Pixabay / mojzagrebinfo

Now let us look at this another way. Let us say that each year you had to perform each of these tasks in succession instead of in little daily or weekly increments that you do not think about, stopping only to sleep for your requisite 7.5 hours, but spending every other waking moment performing each particular task. What would it look like over the course of the year?

- From January 1st-24th you would spend all of your time simply driving to and from work — by yourself (since most North Americans drive by themselves in their car) and during three of those days you would spend all your waking hours completely stuck in traffic!

- From January 25th to May 20th you would work 16-hour days in a job that you probably do not like.[4]

- From May 21st – July 31st you would watch TV continuously — much of it alone and most of it barely entertaining — and a good two solid weeks will be just commercials!

- August 1st – August 20th you will spend in the bathroom, doing whatever it is you do in there!

- August 21st – September 10th you will spend time doing chores including shopping, cleaning, doctor visits and other errands, none of which you wanted to do in the first place!

[4] Most polls in the US show less than 40 percent job satisfaction numbers.

Now wait right there. It is now September 10th. Summer's over and fall has arrived and you still have not spent any quality time with your kids, your spouse or for yourself. And sadly, when you do carve out those times, you end up with less than a month for each. What is wrong with that picture?

How do you spend your time? If these were your patterns, would you make profound changes on your own behalf or for your kids? If you learned that you spent a significant portion of your time in ways that also used considerable energy and increased your ecological footprint, would you find it easier to change? When you look at your time-use patterns, ask yourself how your job choice affects your time. How does where you live affect the hours you spend doing things you do not want to do (such as commute)? Are there activities you would like to be able to spend more time doing? The key is to be aware of things that take time and have a time-oriented ripple effect, drawing on our physical and emotional reserves and making us less effective in other areas.

The sad reality is that we do not notice life passing us by when it does so in little increments. As a result, we tend to make less time for the really important things because we are busy frittering away time on the mundane — what Antoine De Saint-Exupéry calls "matters of consequence."

If you learned that you spent a significant portion of your time in ways that also used considerable energy and increased your ecological footprint, would you find it easier to change?

One is reminded of the life lesson summarized and passed around in recent years via email, in which a professor stands before his classroom with a large vessel, a pile of rocks, a bag of sand and a pitcher of water. He fills the vessel to capacity with rocks, then asks the students if it is full. "Yes," they reply. "No more rocks will fit." He then adds sand, which fills the spaces between the rocks. "Is it full now?" he asks. "Yes, now it is full," the students say. Finally, he adds water, which spreads easily throughout the sand. "Now this vessel is full," he announces. "The moral here is clear: we must start by taking care of the big things in life — family, friends, our health, our well-being — because there will always be room for the little things, as they can take up the remaining spaces."

What to Do?

The sustainability crisis today is a lifestyle crisis, as the ecological problems we face are caused largely by the little decisions millions of us make each day. Yes, consumerism has played a large part, but perhaps just as insidious are our societal patterns that rob us of time while simultane-

> "To my mind, the idea that doing the dishes is unpleasant can occur only when you are not doing them. Once you are standing in front of the sink with your sleeves rolled up and your hands in warm water, it really is not so bad. I enjoy taking my time with each dish, being fully aware of the dish, the water, and each movement of my hands. I know that if I hurry in order to go and have a cup of tea, the time will be unpleasant and not worth living. That would be a pity, for each minute, each second of life is a miracle." - Thich Nhat Hanh

ously causing great environmental impact. We are pulled away from our family lives, civic organizations, community involvement and activities that keep us grounded.

When we have opportunities or are forced to make lifestyle changes — what we do, where we live, how we get from one place to another — and consider the effects our choices have on the environment and our well-being, the connection between time parasitics and sustainability becomes clear. Most activities that eat away at our time also create an environmental burden. For example, the average suburban resident living in a detached home and commuting by car has an ecological footprint almost three times that of his urban counterpart who lives in an apartment and either walks or takes public transportation to work.

Obviously, it is not possible for each environmentally-aware individual to make radical changes all at once. The good news is that we can accomplish many of the same goals by using the nested problem solving approach.

NESTED PROBLEM SOLVING

Every once in a while, we make decisions that seem particularly sound — decisions made in a moment of grace that help solve multiple problems at once. I like to call this type of solution nested problem solving, as individual answers nest within others.

With practice, nested problem solving can become an everyday methodology in and of itself and it has the potential to greatly increase the quality of life we all seek. Once we become aware of the interconnectedness of our daily habits, our ability to manage time and the ecological impact of our decisions, nested solutions come more easily. Please note that this is not the same thing as "multi-tasking," which is merely doing different things at the same time — usually none of it as well as you could do if you focused! Nested problem solving focuses on pairing or merging activities that are synergistic and enhance the result or the enjoyment in doing them. Truly nested solutions tend to be simultaneously good for our health, our pocketbooks and the environment. These solutions are a complete reversal from many habits that cost us a lot, have great environmental burdens and contribute to poor health and leave us with nested problems to be solved!

Nested solutions may be cultivated using such simple tools as daily to-do lists. I, for one, am a relentless list maker. I like to take a few moments in the evening to jot down the key tasks I know I need to accomplish the following day so that, wherever possible, I can group the items on my list into logical categories. This option helps cut down on wasted time, and helps me stay on track.[5] This type of system does not work for everyone, but anyone who wants to streamline time management can find his or her most effective method of nesting solutions.[6]

> Obviously, it is not possible for each environmentally-aware individual to make radical changes all at once. The good news is that we can accomplish many of the same goals by using the nested problem solving approach.

They can also be cultivated by taking the time to reflect on all possible consequences that may occur from the action or task in question and asking "Is there a better way to approach this task that is healthier, more ecologically sound and inexpensive?" It requires a willingness to measure and understand the impacts of the current paradigm before simply changing it.

Naturally, the hardest part of the process is coming up with the solution, but most people are creative enough to come up with several appropriate solutions as soon as they broaden the context.

Unfortunately, many people are stuck in an all too common pattern, a spiraling of interconnected problems that leads to negative feedback loops. For example, the busy career person with no time to cook rarely eats at home — ironically spending almost the same time traveling to and from places to eat, often choosing unhealthy and environmentally disastrous fast food or packaged foods all the while spending at least twice the amount of money for nutritionally diminished fare. The person stuck in this pattern ends up needing to work more to pay for the habit of eating out and the stressful, wasteful cycle continues.

---

5 Something for the right-brain thinker to work on and learn from the left-brain!
6 For more on the power of list making see the book by Atul Guwande called the Checklist Manifesto.

> Making risotto is a directive to slow down, allow time to think and become proactive rather than reactive to our daily routines. Amazing things happen when we turn down our energy levels and do things more slowly and deliberately.

We need to look for synergistic activities or synergistic ways of accomplishing our goals. The Buddhist Thich Nhat Hahn talks about using the mundane to practice the profound, not by multi-tasking but actually by focusing on the task at hand. As he says, "When you are doing the dishes, you should be doing the dishes!" Mindfulness produces its own nested solutions.

MAKING RISOTTO

Whenever I can, I take the time to cook an incredibly elaborate meal at home. I especially enjoy the act of chopping and preparing the ingredients, relishing the fresh raw scent of vegetables, onions and garlic on my hands. Although we have a garlic press, I do not use it in the preparation of one of these feasts, as I prefer to work by hand with an extra sharp knife cutting and slicing and setting each ingredient aside until I have a beautiful tray ready for cooking. For me, these culinary projects are all about delving fully and completely into the task of preparing food for my family and enjoying the process of turning raw ingredients into melded and enriched tastes through cooking. I simply lose myself in it, and it makes for a powerful metaphor in the idea of nested problem solving. While cooking "slow food," I am:

- Pursuing a treasured leisure activity
- Allowing myself time for reflection and stress relief
- Sharing this work (and the fruits of the labor) with loved ones
- Contributing to my health by using quality organic ingredients
- Reducing my environmental footprint, since hand-prepared, seasonal and locally sourced meals have less of an environmental impact than "quick and simple" packaged dishes with ingredients from all corners of the planet

One of my best friends, who has seen me in my soiled apron and who shares similar appreciations for cooking, describes the process of taking the time to do things right as "making risotto." I now use the phrase as

Photo: Pixabay / mquadrelli0

a metaphor for describing the action of losing yourself in any function that promotes quality of life and serves as a nested solution for health, environmental benefit and human interaction. For me, "making risotto" can be as simple as taking a long walk with my dog. Sometimes it is sitting down with a cup of tea and reading a good book for an hour instead of watching television. Making risotto is a directive to slow down, allow time to think and become proactive rather than reactive to our daily routines. Amazing things happen when we turn down our energy levels and do things more slowly and deliberately.

Needless to say, making risotto is a metaphor for green living. In the proverbial rat race, there is little time for anything but consumption and so-called progress. We are reactive rather than proactive, which means we rarely have the time to craft elegant and intelligent solutions.

And yet in the coming years, to address the challenges we will surely face, it is imperative that we have the time to create such compelling solutions. Mastering the "nested time on the brain's right side" becomes essential. ∎

ECOLOGICAL *ORDNUNG* AND THE EVALUATION OF TECHNOLOGY

Showing Restraint in an Unrestrained World

"It is not enough that you should understand about applied science in order that your work may increase man's blessings. Concern for the man himself and his fate must always form the chief interest of all technical endeavors; concern for the great unsolved problems of the organization of labor and the distribution of goods in order that the creations of our mind shall be a blessing and not a curse to mankind. Never forget this in the midst of your diagrams and equations."

Albert Einstein, 1931

What is the first image that pops into your head when you think of Amish communities? Horse-drawn buggies? Barn raisings? Interiors bathed in candlelight? Hand-sewn quilts?

If you know nothing else about the Amish way of life, you are likely familiar with its slower-than-mainstream embrace of modern conveniences. Though you are mistaken if you assume that the Amish reject technology outright. Horse-drawn buggies often have electric taillights, and cordless drills are sometimes used at barn raisings. Why? Because when the Amish decide that the advantages of a technology outweigh its disadvantages, they carefully and thoughtfully introduce that technology into the framework of their society. If, however, a technology poses potential negative consequences to their culture or beliefs — such as the use of sewing machines, which might threaten the sense of community and craftsmanship that are characteristic of a quilting circle — then the device is deemed undesirable.

The key is in the deliberation, and the deliberation stems from the *Ordnung*.

Ordnung is a German word that conveys the concept of order, discipline or rule. Ordnung is also the expression commonly used to define the Amish and Mennonite ways of life. In these cultures, the Ordnung is an unwritten set of rules and regulations that helps to protect the communities' time-honored traditions, including those that reject many modern conveniences. The Ordnung is designed to maintain a balance between the old and the new, to "slow or prevent change if a given technology is seen to be a threat."[1] The Amish feel that some modern technologies might diminish one's connections to family, community and the value of hard work.

It is remarkable that the North American Amish have been able to maintain their preferred pace of life and commitment to a non-consumerist culture while being literally surrounded by the world's most consumer-oriented, technology-hungry and change-driven societies.

The *Ordnung* guides the Amish to take the time to make thoughtful decisions when it comes to what they want for themselves and for their communities, regardless of outside influences. It should remind the rest of us that such mindfulness is possible. The Amish have proven that societies of people can come together to make collective choices about how technology, materials, products and processes affect culture.

When it comes to finding the sweet spot between indulgence and restraint, we can learn much from the Amish *Ordnung* — even if we do not share their particular ideals or a desire to slow the pace of change to the extent that they do.

---

1   amishamerica.com/do-amish-use-technology

> "The Amish blueprint for expected behavior, called the Ordnung, regulates private, public and ceremonial life. Ordnung... is best thought of as an ordering of the whole way of life... a code of conduct which the church maintains by tradition rather than by systematic or explicit rules... The Ordnung evolved gradually over the decades as the church sought to strike a delicate balance between tradition and change."

- Donald B. Kraybill, *The Riddle of Amish Culture*

In our increasingly fast-paced, sometimes frantic, modern world, we are bombarded with technological innovations and new products that are quickly made obsolete by improved versions, which then are eclipsed by even newer approaches. There seems to be virtually no end to what we can invent and mechanize, so we continue to innovate because we can, not necessarily because we need to, or should. As recently as 25 years ago, in-home computers were relatively rare, and WiFi was non-existent. Today, many adults and children cannot imagine going a day without using a computer. In the same time period, telephones have lost their rotary dials and the curly cords that once tethered them to kitchen walls; phones are now "smart" and have found their way into the pockets and purses of people around the world — including in developing nations. Looking back even 100 years, a mere blip on the timeline of human existence, the change has been nothing less than revolutionary, encompassing the wholesale reinvention of modern civilization., transforming communications, education, medicine, transportation, entertainment and more. We have only in the last few decades begun to understand that some of our technologies are now changing the entire fabric of life on the planet and leading to potentially catastrophic pollution, species loss and climate change.

Admittedly, many of these changes have benefited humankind, at least in the short term. I do believe, for example, that the innovations of Silicon Valley and other global tech hubs, while not completely innocent, are generally helping move us toward a better world by informing us and bringing us closer together. That said, other technologies, including the energy sources that are powering the computer and telecommunications revolutions, have had significant negative and unintended consequences.

Photo: Flickr Creative Commons / ProgressOhio

What is clear, regardless of the sector or technology, is that we have no reliable checks and balances in place that encourage us to pause and ask: Should we do this? Is this a good idea for the betterment of humanity?

Unfortunately, there are many moments in human history where I wish we had been able to call upon a system of safeguards and had decided not to go forward with a technology. Learning how to split the atom provided the knowledge to invent nuclear power, but it also led to its notorious byproduct, the atomic bomb. I would argue that this is a genie most of humanity wishes it could put back in the bottle. Granted there are some positive applications for the technologies that followed; however, too many have suffered and died because of this technology to justify the short-term advantages, and too much is at stake to risk future accidents and violence.

Another example of technology that the world would be better off without is hydraulic fracturing to extract natural gas. "Fracking" is already causing significant long-term problems affecting groundwater in many locations, and the catastrophic ecological effects on the water table and nearby aquifers may not be fully known for generations. And what of the booming chemical, pesticide and pharmaceutical industries, which

Photo: Unsplash / Crew

present selected advantages (particularly related to health and longevity) but have profound effects on the food chain and potentially on life itself? Genetically modified organisms and foods, and countless other "discoveries," are further examples of innovations that are foisted upon us with little to no rigorous deliberation and debate. The same could be said about many other seemingly innocuous technologies that permeate our communities and our daily lives.

The very things that bind us together culturally — the types of connections people have to one another and to nature, which the Amish work so hard to protect — are the things that technology has the power to remove from our social framework. Televisions, computers and cell phones work together to dull us as they pull us apart, separating us from one another physically and socially. Those of us who exist with modern conveniences spend a disturbing amount of our time in virtual worlds where the real is supplanted by the impersonal. We've uploaded our collective knowledge to "the cloud," but it is a soulless source of human intelligence and experience. What will be the long-term effect on humanity from the generations that spend more time interacting with technological devices rather than directly with people and other living things?

"In recent years social scientists have framed concerns about the changing character of American society in terms of the concept of 'social capital.' By analogy with notions of physical capital and human capital – tools and training that enhance individual productivity – the core idea of social capital theory is that social networks have value. Just as a screwdriver (physical capital) or a college education (human capital) can increase productivity (both individual and collective), so too social contacts affect the productivity of individuals and groups. ...Social capital turns out to have forceful, even quantifiable effects on many different aspects of our lives. What is at stake is not merely warm, cuddly feelings or frissons of community pride. We shall review hard evidence that our schools and neighborhoods don't work so well when community bonds slacken, that our economy, our democracy, and even our health and happiness depend on adequate stocks of social capital."

- Robert D. Putnam, *Bowling Alone: The Collapse and Revival of American Community*

When it comes to technological innovation, there is no democratic system through which big-picture questions are asked and holistic decisions are made. Such exploration is typically reserved for the corporations and shareholders that will benefit materially once a new discovery is broadly implemented. The "deciders" in society tend to be corporate entities, boards that take action according to market dynamics rather than human or ecological consequences. We, the consumers, rarely have a say in what is foisted upon us, nor do those at-risk populations who stand to suffer the most through poverty, hunger or displacement in the wake of these market successes. The argument that consumers in a free market economy have the power to accept or reject any product doesn't hold up here for several reasons: first, it is not enough to opt out of a purchase decision when the product and/or its use changes the very fabric of society like technological secondhand smoke; second, the market serves as a false proxy when it comes to sweeping decisions made by few but affecting many; and third, powerful product marketing campaigns are very persuasive in getting people to buy things that might not even be good for them, although consumers might not see the ill effects until years or decades later.

This process is not democratic; it is tyranny under the guise of democracy.

We live in an age of technological heroism, in which inventors and forward-thinking companies are feted before the real or potential impacts of their discoveries are truly considered. The present day economy is being built around a technological and mechanistic future, to the extent that even questioning the wisdom of this approach makes a person seem old fashioned. Do those of us who are concerned about the continuing march of technology and manufactured goods deserve to be labeled as out of touch, or is there a way to find balance between celebrating the positive contributions of technology while recognizing that not all technological innovations should be accepted without first applying the precautionary principle?

My own choices (my personal *Ordnung*) help illustrate the complex nature of this discussion, as I am actually a classic early adopter of new technology. Most of the time, I am curious about the latest tools and gadgets — especially those that are designed with beauty and elegance — and intrigued enough by them to want to explore.

If the Amish Ordnung is strong enough to keep technology at bay for communities completely surrounded by the modern world, why can't the rest of us adopt even a partial set of guidelines that would fundamentally assist us in evaluating the impact of some of our own ideas?

But I always ask two important qualitative questions while weighing the value of any new technology, the answers to which determine whether I will embrace the innovation enthusiastically or resist it actively:

1. Does the technology have the capacity to enrich my life or that of my family in some way?

2. Does the technology have the capacity to improve the world on an environmental, social or cultural basis, or will it diminish it?

I jumped on the iPod bandwagon from the very beginning and loved the experience of having a diversity of music at my fingertips, delivered by a device that is beautiful, and efficient. I believe the technology brought joy to people by exposing more individuals to more music and culture. At the same time, my wife and I try to limit our children's screen time and nurture their connections to the natural environment because we want them to experience the critical balance that prioritizes nature over technology. Admittedly, this is a constant battle.

Also, I was such an early proponent of electric cars that I owned one (Corbin Sparrow) before the technology had really been refined. I believe so strongly in the need to do away with the internal combustion engine and the oil industry that underlies it that I wanted to lend my support to a relatively untested approach even if it meant purchasing a vehicle that wasn't really ready for prime time.

The arc of human invention offers an interesting historical backdrop. Early humans were subject to the varying forces of nature, thus early inventions typically worked in concert with natural rhythms and systems. Given that balance, humans' impact on the environment for most of our evolutionary history was light. But as we "advanced" our technologies, we pulled ourselves and our material inventions further from nature to the point of exploitation, disconnecting us from our responsibilities as the planet's stewards. Given both the rate of change and the severe environmental consequences that are emerging, we now need to selectively realign our technologies and products in ways that allow us to honor our inventive instincts and our stewardship responsibilities at the same time.

We currently have very few systems in place that help us filter what we unleash on the world. If we can invent, build, automate or digitize it, we go for it, engaging in almost no intelligent societal discourse about the

Photo: Unsplash / William Iven

Photo: Flickr Creative Commons / IAEA Imagebank

wisdom of doing so. The potential consequences and ramifications of our inventions go more or less unaddressed. There is a certain underlying assumption that the crunching forward motion of technological innovation is inevitable, that we have no say in the matter, that all things new are better than what came before.

We now need to selectively realign our technologies and products in ways that allow us to honor our inventive instincts and our stewardship responsibilities at the same time, given both the rate of change and the severe environmental consequences that are emerging. We must be more deliberate and thoughtful in our approach to technological progress, incorporating healthy civic dialogue that allow us to question: Does this innovation serve the greater human and environmental good? To repeat something my father used to always say to me, "Just because you can do something doesn't give you the right to do it."

One thing we know to be true is that the rate of change will keep increasing as technology serves itself before it serves us. So we need to advocate for life and people and culture as we map out our technological future, stopping to ask: What will be the impacts of our inventions? How can we be more strategic with what we create? Are there ways to achieve the same result with a regenerative rather than degenerative series of impacts? How can we pursue a modern lifestyle while also healing so much of the world we've harmed? Do we really want a future where everything is done for us, or one in which our cities, buildings, materials and products crowd out the natural world?

In his book *What Are People For?*, author and poet Wendell Berry ponders where our automated society will eventually take us. If we end up capable of building machines so sophisticated that everything could be mechanized, would we? Is that what we really want? Are we striving for a society that makes humans extraneous? Berry's position, of course, is that to be human means to have purpose, to stay engaged, to know the satisfaction of creating something with one's own hands. He argues that idleness is problematic for the human species, yet our technological pursuits make us increasingly idle.

> Somewhere along our path toward modernity, we decided that restraint was antiquated.

What's missing is a particular type of *Ordnung* — cultural and ecological — that would help modern societies assess technologies and products according to how the innovations may benefit living things, not just how they serve the forward march of progress or the pocketbooks of a few. If the Amish *Ordnung* is strong enough to keep technology at bay for communities completely surrounded by the modern world, why can't the rest of us adopt even a partial set of guidelines that would fundamentally assist us in evaluating the impact of some of our own ideas?

Such a system would offer us a set of sound principles and metrics by which to guide our actions thoughtfully — built around a shared vision of the future we all wish to see. There has to be discernment, and the process has to be democratic and transparent.

Any technologies or materials that present even modest environmental impact should be subject to a true, and often slow, scientific and democratic review, as should any innovation with potentially broad cultural implications. At the same time, we should accelerate the progress of technologies that advance education, foster global citizenship and elevate impoverished cultures.

The key is finding balance — putting the brakes on the potentially damaging technologies while punching the accelerator on the universally beneficial ones. It will not be easy, and we will make many mistakes along the way, but what better use for our democracy than encouraging its citizens to really think through the consequences of its actions? Some good innovations may end up being unintentionally stifled, but only in service to the greater good. Many "good" technologies are already stymied through an unfair economic system.

Photo: Pixabay / JoeKeim

An ecological *Ordnung* will help to minimize or avoid future technological disasters like the ones we've already created (Fukushima comes to mind). Somewhere along our path toward modernity, we decided that restraint was antiquated. As a result, we are speeding through the modern era, paying little attention to the future we are mapping out for ourselves.

There is no black and white solution to the issue of managing human technological innovation. We certainly can't forget what we've learned how to do. However, now that the stakes are as high as they are and the rate of change so rapid, the time has come for us to be more deliberate when we evaluate what types of technologies we can and should weave into our societal framework. We need to approach technology from a more mature perspective, taking the time to explore the long-term implications of our discoveries from every social and environmental angle.

Because technology is here supposedly to serve us and not to diminish us, the underlying question must always be: Does this human construction create positive conditions for life? Our modern inventions have been made possible by the countless others that preceded them. The idea that any one invention is truly novel is likely untrue — more accurately, we have a system where all the benefit goes to the first to patent instead of to the culture that makes innovation possible. The collective wisdom of humans across all generations and in all societies has made these innovations possible, so it is only right for all of humanity to benefit from what technology has to offer. The reverse, then, is also true: technology that could harm living species should be up to all of us to judge, and anything that exploits people or the environment should be very difficult to get approved.

We already impose certain limits on our capabilities. Drugs are subject to FDA approval. Products are subject to UL safety listings. Manufacturers are subject to EPA and other guidelines. These examples show that we sometimes understand the wisdom of restraint (usually only after some sort of disaster). We need to extend deeper and have similarly intelligent dialogue about a broader range of topics.

I acknowledge the inherent challenges in finding the balance between invention and oversight, but a society without restraint is not a society at all. We apply restraint when we parent, when we obey laws, when we behave civilly in public. There are certain rules we know to follow and limits we know to observe; honoring such boundaries enables us to protect others and ourselves while retaining our places in civilized society. It is generally understood that no one person's rights should impede the rights of others. Doesn't nature deserve the same treatment? Shouldn't we restrain our actions that threaten other living systems?

I am encouraged by the availability of information in the digital age because it democratizes knowledge in (mostly) positive ways and is an example of the type of technology that should not be overly constrained. Used wisely and productively, information that is truly available to all — regardless of social, gender, economic, ethnic or geographic distinctions — can only enhance the enlightenment of the human race, freeing those held captive by ignorance and isolation. We should utilize technological channels to enable full transparency of those decisions that are made by a few but affect the masses. Leaders from the public and private sectors would no longer be able to take far-reaching action without first hearing from the populations that might experience some impact.

Following the same logic, information technology should be used to educate the human race — the whole human race. The better educated we all are, the better we will be able to make informed decisions about things that affect all of us. A broad knowledge base made available to all would create global communities of well-rounded generalists, empowering people to grasp the nuances and the measurable facts of important issues.

> "We are called to be architects of the future, not its victims. [The challenge is] to make the world work for 100% of humanity in the shortest possible time, with spontaneous cooperation and without ecological damage or disadvantage of anyone."
>
> - Buckminster Fuller

The less we have to rely on the opinions of a handful of experts, the more democratic and sane our global decision-making process can become.

Our modern-day *Ordnung* could inform our collective decisions with regard to technology. In its ideal, such a standard — a set of simple criteria, broadly applied — would guide us toward innovations, systems and solutions that:

- have an impact only where we want them to;
- have largely predictable outcomes;
- will have positive effects on our culture and way of life;
- will not have adverse effects on the poor, the disadvantaged, children and future generations;
- do not impoverish or enslave any populations;
- have no lasting and significant undesirable effects on other species (from the plankton to the whale);
- cannot "get away" from us or "escape" into other systems like invasives;
- offer potential side effects that are proportionally smaller than the benefits;
- stay within the boundaries of disconnect that describes our ability to understand and relate to the scale of the invention, technology or system;
- require the approval of a diverse assembly, with a focus on seniority and wisdom, ensuring the input of those who can remember what came before.

We can learn important lessons from the Amish and their *Ordnung* when it comes to simplifying, connecting to nature and resisting inevitability. They have proven that their belief system works harder for them than technology ever could.

Individually and collectively, we have both a choice and a voice. It is incumbent upon us to use both to question the uncontrolled technological and mechanistic takeover of our modern societies, lest we habituate this passivity to the point of surrender. With surrender, I fear, will come a world devoid of natural, organic, living systems.

We can become a regenerative species with the power and the technological acumen to create a living future. To reach our potential as true global stewards, we must place limits upon ourselves when our discoveries have potential negative impacts on living species. Nothing with the capacity to broadly affect people or nature should be considered unstoppable. If a technological or material innovation threatens basic human rights or delicate ecosystems, it should never be thought of as inevitable. Our role is not to use technology to elevate ourselves above nature, but to elevate the human experience within the context of a natural world.

We are smart enough to question our own brilliance and put it to its sanest use. We will only achieve a living future if we put our inventions to work to protect the living present. ■

> **"[Design Science is] the effective application of the principles of science to the conscious design of our total environment in order to help make the earth's finite resources meet the needs of all humanity without disrupting the ecological processes of the planet."**
>
> **- Buckminster Fuller**

A LIVING TRANSPORTATION FUTURE

Getting Around in a Regenerative Society

ORIGINALLY PUBLISHED 2014

JASON F. MCLENNAN 161

"You never change things by fighting the existing reality. To change something, build a new model that makes the existing model obsolete."

Buckminster Fuller

Humans have always been on the move. In prehistoric times, getting from one place to the next was a matter of survival as we followed the herds, weather and seasons. For thousands of years, we moved only by foot. Several thousand years ago, a small portion of humanity was aided by beasts of burden and early sailing vessels to enable travel farther and farther afield.

The modern story is all too familiar: we've progressed to the point where our modes of transportation — our cars, buses, trains and planes — are major contributors to the decline of the planet's life support systems. The more we travel, the more we imperil the planet's future. Humans have introduced transportation technologies that threaten the health of people, the environment, our communities and our very quality of life.

If we had been blessed with a more critical foresight, perhaps we would have stopped and asked more questions, been more objective, and questioned the long-term impacts of each new technology on people, culture and the environment. Instead, we continue to forge ahead in the name of progress, innovating our way forward, overly proud of our accomplishments in the pursuit of going farther, faster.

So here we are in the 21st century, despite futuristic predictions of how we'd get around by now,[1] living in a highly polluting, dangerous and culture-eroding society that is dominated by automobiles, the logical outcome of an early 20th century technology. As we drive blissfully forward while staring blankly at our dwindling supplies of oil, it does little good to bemoan past decisions to build the interstate systems, suburban landscapes and unending sprawl that have so disconnected us from nature and from each other.

It is tempting to wish that we could go back a hundred years, armed with our current knowledge, and ask the people who were just setting out on this path, "What would you think of creating a transportation paradigm that will destroy city patterns and community life, poison the environment, be responsible for thousands of accidental deaths and injuries each year, and require a fuel source that is so scarce and unevenly distributed that it will pit armies from various continents against one another, causing the deaths of untold innocents?" We'd like to think that no person would have embraced such a model because it makes no sense, though the allure of profit and speed would likely still prevail. Yet, we find ourselves today in the midst of that nonsensical mess; we can't go back in time, but our past decisions have bound us to the current paradigm.

---

1 It was predicted in the fifties that we'd live in outer space, in moon colonies and travel by nuclear powered vessels by now.

WHAT IS POSSIBLE?

What we've learned time and time again is that guilt is a poor motivator for change. We've known about the negative impacts of our current transportation paradigm for at least four decades. We've compiled the stats and we've educated people on alternatives, yet year-in and year-out, we lose ground because we haven't offered a compelling alternative that creates the same levels of comfort and convenience that people seek in any transportation paradigm.

The Institute is providing a new vision that is beginning to reshape the conversation around buildings — Living Buildings that are beautiful, inspiring, more comfortable, healthier, and economically justifiable. Living Buildings have no future if they are ugly, provide occupant discomfort or are cost-prohibitive. If we want our transportation paradigm to change, the same must happen. The solutions, like with Living Buildings, must be holistic and interconnected, and they must address the problems of entire underlying systems, not just the individual parts.

It's time to plan for a healthy, compelling alternative: a living, regenerative transportation network that will carry us into the future. As is true with so many sustainable solutions, we have the technology now to achieve this goal, so this is not a matter of having to wait for new inventions (although certainly refinements are needed to further improve all aspects of the system). We simply need to embrace and reimagine the ideas we've already begun to develop. For example, bicycles have always been relevant as a major component of our transportation future,

> **The more we travel, the more we imperil the planet's future.**

and we've already created electric cars and trains that function beautifully. Now is the time to think bigger, imagining sustainable systems and policies that will meet everybody's transportation needs without diminishing the planet's life support systems. Some of our solutions may not be elegant at first, but we continually learn the most from our failures.

Switching infrastructure systems is never easy, but it is always possible, and success typically depends primarily on overcoming cultural and attitudinal barriers, which can only be done if the paradigm introduced offers a more compelling vision and promise than the one it is intended to replace. Converting to a revolutionary transportation paradigm will yield winners and losers, just as was true when we transitioned from the horse to the automobile. When the automobile was introduced, it was unfathomable that this unreliable, loud transportation technology could ever prevail without road, fuel and repair networks. Experts of the day thought that it could never replace the horse and buggy. But within two decades the automobile had done just that, and all the systems needed to sustain the auto culture

EVOLUTION OF HUMAN TRANSPORTATION

200,000 BC
The Foot Era
Humans first relied on our own bodies to get us where we needed to go. This phase lasted for most of human history.

10,000 BC
The Animal Era:
Next, we turned to other living things to help move us and our cargo.

5,000 BC
The Winds and Currents Era:
Our early transportation machines called on energy generated by the air and the water. They were essentially non-polluting, but at the whim of nature.

1800–1900s
The Rail and Streetcar Era
Then our innovations (and the materials required to build them) began to pollute as we took 'control' of transportation future — the steam era began.

1900s
The Automobile and Airplane Era
In the name of convenience, our modern methods have begun to alter the climate of our planet and sicken us as a species. Soon, we will run out of the fuel required to power these machines. The era of the internal combustion engine.

2000s
The Regenerative Transportation Era
A healthy human transportation future, relying on technologies that already exist, is possible. We are only now getting glimpses of this era's possibilities.

JASON F. MCLENNAN

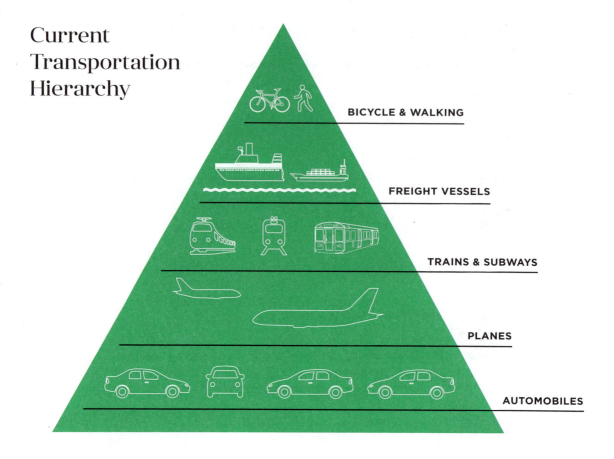

The above pyramid shows the emphasis we place on our current modes of transportation. The most polluting forms of travel at the base of the pyramid and the most regenerative at the top with the least use.

were in place. Money and profit potential drove much of the change (and sometimes political scandal), and that's still true today — so a new vision must excite people economically and experientially.

It is my belief that framing a living transportation future in a compelling fashion will succeed if we follow the same principles required to create a living building future. In fact, the next iteration of the Living Building Challenge, version 3.0, will more fully integrate the concept of transportation. In other words, the goals of the new paradigm must meet the same performance requirements we demand from living buildings. We imagine the need for a transportation future that is socially just, culturally rich, and ecologically restorative, where every single act of locomotion helps regenerate and restore our communities and the ecology underpinning them.

When the automobile was introduced, it was unfathomable that this unreliable, loud transportation technology could ever prevail without road, fuel and repair networks.

A CHALLENGING ADVENTURE

The International Living Future Institute was inspired to tackle the topic of regenerative transportation in part because of our work with the historic 1913 schooner *Adventuress*, which is now used for environmental and maritime education in the waters surrounding Seattle. As part of its centennial restoration, *Adventuress* is being refurbished according to the framework of the Living Building Challenge. This inspirational effort has proven that the principles of the Challenge can apply just as readily to the vessels that move us around as they do to the built environment.

UNDERSTANDING THE OLD AND NEW PARADIGMS.

Current Transportation Paradigm

Today, we draw disproportionately on systems whose damaging effects far outweigh their benefits.

A Living Transportation Paradigm

By making human- and renewably-powered methods of transportation the norm, and only rarely relying on resource-hungry machines, we will flip the old system on its head.

POWER TO THE PEDAL

When it comes to transportation, one of the greatest paradigm-busting examples is the ELF pedal/solar hybrid vehicle. Made by Organic Transit in Durham, North Carolina, the ELF delivers the mobility of a bicycle with the added boost of an electric assist. Built to be ridden like any standard bike, the ELF's rooftop solar panels provide enough supplemental clean power to carry its rider/driver at speeds of up to 30 mph. The ELF is a bike first and foremost. But when the circumstances, terrain or dress code require supplemental strength, it can become a renewably motorized vehicle. At just 95 pounds, the ELF gets the equivalent of 1,800

We imagine the need for a transportation future that is socially just, culturally rich, and ecologically restorative, where every single act of locomotion helps regenerate and restore our communities and the ecology underpinning them.

miles per gallon (even though it requires not a drop of fuel). Referred to by various early reviewers as a "sunbike," a "solar tricycle" and "the next big thing for eco-commuters," the ELF shows what is possible when change is required. I, for one, am looking forward to going for a spin. I am the proud owner of an ELF and will use it for miscellaneous commuting and short in-town travel. It's still a bit rough around the edges in its 1.0 version — but it holds great promise as a new class of vehicles that could begin to fully dominate the transportation scene. Imagine if we used vehicles like this for the majority of our in-town commuting. We'd be healthier and safer, have more fun commuting, and our cities could begin to be reshaped around a more human scale.

REINVENTING THE CAR

By now, most environmentally-aware consumers are familiar with Tesla Motors and the revolutionary Tesla all-electric luxury sedan. While Tesla was not the first company to offer an electric automobile by any stretch (indeed, I owned an early Corbin Sparrow for ten years), it has taken things to a new level with its powerful design, incredible battery technology and perhaps most importantly with its growing network of Supercharger stations. Until now, an electric car's utility was limited to its range. They offered an ideal way to travel short distances but were not a realistic option for longer journeys and therefore unpractical for most people. Even when I owned my electric car, I still had to have a second gas vehicle for longer trips.

Tesla is changing the paradigm, first by extending the range to a couple of hundred miles per trip. The company's newly emerging Supercharger stations are now cropping up throughout the country, with more on the way. (As of this writing, the company website lists locations in most U.S. and Canadian metropolitan areas and expects to have enough stations in place by next year to serve 80 percent of those countries' residents.) A Tesla sedan can take a full 120kW charge in less than 30 minutes, giving the car up to another 300 miles in range, essentially guaranteeing free energy. Each station offers or is situated near other amenities, so travelers can eat, shop or connect with other travelers while their cars repower.

The result is a safe, gorgeous, clean-powered vehicle that can take its passengers farther afield without doing damage along the way. While I still believe in minimizing the number of automobiles on the road due to their significant negative impacts on urban form and safety, the Tesla model and its supercharging network is, in my opinion, the start of a revolution. Imagine our country without the need for gas stations, super tankers, oil refineries, without air pollution and not caught up in Middle Eastern wars! Tesla is singlehandedly creating a system that could make the existing paradigm obsolete. With enough traction, this system will be rapidly copied and in a couple of decades we could be completely weaned from oil.[2]

A LOOK AT A NEW ERA

I envision a regenerative transportation era that prioritizes humans and our communities, not cars and their freeways. To make this vision work, our cities have to change. Since societies are built around their dominant form(s) of transportation, it's time to start rebuilding our cities with healthier ways of moving citizens around as a top priority. Let's unpack this idea further:

---

2   Here is a prediction. As the Tesla begins to gain even more market share, expect the oil industries and conventional automakers to begin to work hard to limit and discredit it as a system. Watch carefully for how the media portrays any problems that Tesla has — playing up any accident as potentially a giant fault in the vehicle even though gas powered vehicles routinely have safety problems and aren't held to the same standard.

A Living Transportation Hierarchy

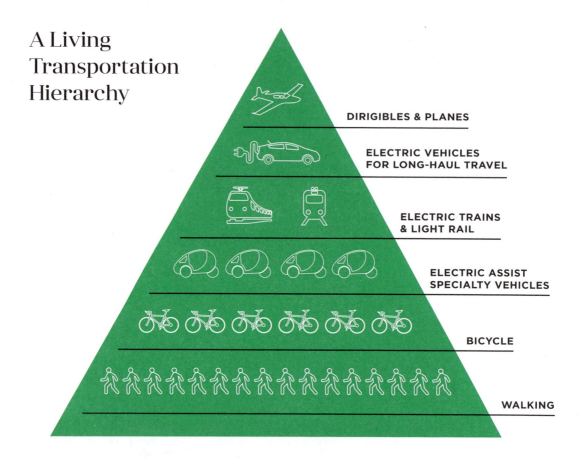

This new hierarchy puts walkable communities as the foundation of our transportation future, followed closely by bicycles, electric assist bikes and vehicles.

First, it is important to understand that it is not enough to simply change the 'mode' of transportation. As much as I admire Tesla and other electric cars, merely replacing all internal combustion engines with electric motors does not get us to the place we seek and indeed can create other challenges, although this is a good early transition step.[3] Electric cars matched with renewable energy-based charging gets us closer, but still does nothing to heal the damage that personal automobile transportation has done to the fabric of our communities. The spatial dynamics of planning around cars and the resulting decentralization of community need to be challenged. Our cities need to planned around the scale of people,

---

[3] You still have to get electricity from somewhere – and if it's from a dirty grid then you've made the problem worse in some areas.

not around giant machines, and the huge swathes of land that have been given over to auto enablement need to be repurposed. A living transportation paradigm requires cities and towns to be planned differently, with the highest priority given to the pedestrian and the cyclist, and the automobile reserved for very specific and specialized transportation needs.

When communities begin removing auto infrastructure they find that it can greatly revitalize the area and allows for a restitching of the urban fabric. The removal of San Francisco's Embarcadero, and the soon-to-be-removed Seattle viaduct, allows for vital reconnection to the waterfront as well as visual and auditory relief. Repurposing abandoned infrastructure can also create new and rich urban experiences, such as the New York Highline (perhaps the best new landscape design since Olmsted), which is now serving as inspiration for many other communities that have abandoned rail and freeway sections.

In place of auto infrastructure we now have greater room for increased density, for daylighting streams and providing landscaped channels for storm water, or even for avenues of urban food production and habitat.

Providing infrastructure for bikes is the top priority; dedicated bike lanes and bike sharing programs like the green bikes in New York City start to reinforce a bike culture similar to one that is so strong in Portland, Oregon, where people of all ages and demographics bike to work each day — rain or shine.[4] We have to support emergent companies like Organic Transit, which themselves are extending the power, utility and climate acceptability of bikes through new vehicle typologies.

The trend of adding light rail, even in currently auto-dominated communities, is highly positive because it makes leaving the auto more viable for people who still need to travel greater distances. A well thought-out grid of light rail allows people to walk, bike, and hop on trains to traverse the city as well as or better than getting into cars. Connecting this grid to an enhanced national rail system (with fast trains) will allow for seamless and enjoyable mid- to long-haul journeys. Funding a national high-speed rail system should be a top political priority. The fact that our nation's trains are so inefficient when compared to those in other countries is embarrassing — and an opportunity missed.

Ultimately, as the transition unfolds over the next couple of decades, our city infrastructure is radically changing — we will have new street standards and street sections, greatly diminished parking requirements, and a human powered and solar powered hierarchy of travel. Let's imagine life in a city with a Living Transportation Paradigm:

---

4 In some communities teens are shunning the normal right of passage of getting their drivers' license in favor of the bike, which is seen as more hip and responsible.

IMAGINE

Imagine you live in a city where the vast majority of people don't own cars — they don't need to, and they don't want to. Sure, there are some cars available because each neighborhood has a 'vehicle hub' where you can rent an electric truck or car on the rare occasion one would be necessary, but the costs associated with car ownership have completely disappeared, along with local air pollution, auto accidents, noise, and the vast parking and auto transportation infrastructure. You were surprised by how quickly the auto paradigm changed once the right systems were in place. All the experts said it couldn't happen, but with a new generation and better transportation models emerging, the transition was quick. Sure, service vehicles — police, fire, ambulances and construction — still exist, and all are now able to navigate more efficiently to their destinations.

With communication technology as advanced as it is, you often work from home, or from parks and cafes, reducing transportation needs considerably. Your work-life balance seems much easier — regaining the hour per day that you used to spend commuting has been wonderful. When you do need to travel to meetings or for other activities, you typically walk or ride your bike. This transition might not have been easy at first, but now it's the most pleasurable part of the day. If it's raining, you might rent a covered electric-assist bike or walk with your umbrella to the light rail stop, which is never more than a few minutes away. Because of this daily pattern, you see and know your neighbors more, you've lost weight, and you feel healthier and more fit. You take greater notice and care of your street, your park, and your doorstep. In general you've slowed down, and you can feel how much less stress there is. You can't help but notice how your community has been greatly strengthened in the last few years. Somehow, even though everyone is going slower, everyone seems to have considerably more time, which many now spend in ways that bring the neighborhood together.

Gone is your long commute, and now even when you do travel farther by train or light rail you can read, socialize, eat or nap. It's no longer something you dread. You've noticed that community revitalization is up in general — fewer tax dollars being drained into road repair and the huge interstate system, which has now been abandoned. The last time you rented a beautiful electric sports car to visit the coast, you noticed that the local roads and the small towns that line them are now healthier, too — no longer bypassed and ignored. Your town's main street and central business district are livelier, with cleaner air and more people walking and spending their money locally. And it's so quiet compared to the old days; you can even hear birds sing downtown! Avenues are no longer

An image of a living future community with a completely re-aligned transportation paradigm.

filled with parking stalls and parking meters but with fruit trees, street furniture and bikes!

On weekends you love to jog along the new habitat corridors, and you notice that others, like you, are healthier. You've read that as obesity has declined, so has the prevalence of diabetes and upper respiratory illnesses. Rates of depression are down, as are crime rates because of more "eyes on the street" and pride of place. You are delighted to hear that the United States, which once had some of the highest health care costs per person of any nation, now has among the lowest. You smile when you think of the demise of giant parking lots, big box retail stores with blank facades, and giant signs that once dominated the auto landscape. Developments like these have all been reimagined — initially materials were repurposed for use in other buildings or redeveloped into dense, walkable villages connected to your community. It's even been two years since you've had to get on a plane, since your train pass grants you access to the entire national network with ease and speed.

You pull your bike into your bike locker and walk up to your porch. Things sure have changed. You are home.

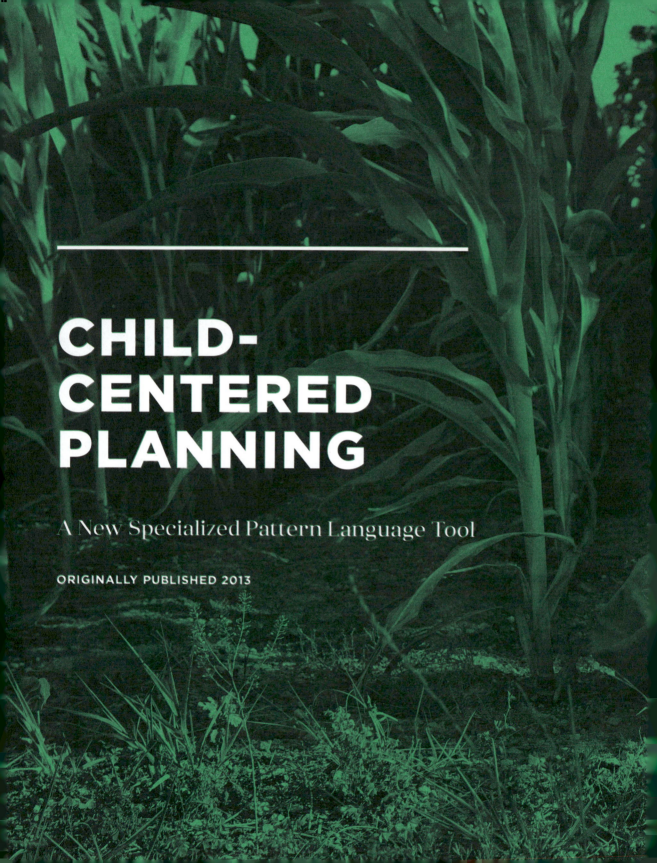

CHILD-CENTERED PLANNING

A New Specialized Pattern Language Tool

ORIGINALLY PUBLISHED 2013

JASON F. MCLENNAN 175

The idea is to help children find their way while making them feel celebrated instead of simply tolerated.

This last year global population crossed the seven billion mark, and within less than two decades another billion are projected to live on planet earth. The hidden statistic is that almost all of the last billion and likely the majority of the next will be city dwellers. It was only in the last several decades that we moved from a predominantly rural civilization to an urban one. As megacities grow, even as small and midsized cities grow around the world, our technologies, especially our cars and other modes of transportation, continue to have the largest impact on the nature of the City: how it looks, functions and is experienced. What's obvious is that nature is continually being squeezed out of our urban experiences, as are the kind of experiences that are good for people. Especially telling is the lack of attention placed on our most vulnerable and important citizens: our children. We might design communities fit for auto transport and auto storage, but too many cities are cruel and inhospitable to our most impressionable.

I have written previously about the wisdom of designing buildings and communities that deeply consider children first as a way of ensuring that communities are well designed for people of all ages. (See "Our Children's Cities: The Logic and Beauty of a Child-Centered Civilization" in my first book in this series titled *Transformational Thought: Radical Ideas to Remake the Built Environment*, 2012.) What can be more important than ensuring that our urban habitats are nurturing and supportive of human development, and that we create environments that maximize human potential?

Recently I returned to my decades-old copy of Christopher Alexander's seminal work, *A Pattern Language*, which had a profound influence on the design world (and on me) following its publication in the late 1970s. With child-centered design on my mind, I began to think about how one might apply an Alexander-esque pattern language to plan children-centric cities

UniverCity Development: From Living Building to Living Community

that are safe, beautiful and enjoyable for children of all ages. After all, if great places share common patterns as Alexander asserts, then great child-oriented communities also should reveal certain patterns that can form the basis of planning.

The beauty of planning cities for their youngest inhabitants stems from the idea's simplicity. Designing places for our most vulnerable citizens allows us to create places that better serve everyone. The focus on the young has particularly strong benefits for the elderly. Rather than constructing communities around the automobile, we should treat our children as our highest priorities. Doing so will keep them safe and keep us sane.

What follows is a preliminary list of 40 patterns that I have identified as necessary for a child-centered community to be successful. Over time we hope to expand and add to this list as an important new design tool for architects, planners and community leaders to use wherever civic engagements are happening.

CHILD-CENTERED PATTERNS

The Child Centered Patterns are organized into the following categories. Many of the patterns relate to multiple categories at the same time, and are especially important.

 Education   Accessibility

 Beauty   Safety

 Resilience   Playfulness

 Connectedness   Joy

 Biophilia   Health

Pattern 1: The Story of Place

Education, Beauty, Resilience, Connectedness, Biophilia

The more children who understand the places where they live, the more committed they will be to celebrating and protecting their regions. In child-centered communities, youth must be taught the social, ecological, climatological and even architectural histories of the areas so that they can fully grasp the complexities—and make the most of the unique offerings—of their homes. Tools such as community weather stations and public interpretive elements will help children place their communities in a global context while rooting them more solidly in place.

Pattern 2: The Child's-Eye View

Beauty, Safety, Connectedness, Accessibility

Respecting a lower ground plane lets us all see what children see. To enhance visibility, safety and beauty, accommodate individuals who stand 3-4 feet tall rather than following the old standard that assumes everyone walks or wheels 5-6 feet off the ground. Sight lines are clearer, barriers are less restricting, and spaces are more open.

Children need a visual connection to the life of the street so that they can see people and nature in vibrant action.

Pattern 3: Humane Scale

Beauty, Safety, Joy, Connectedness, Biophilia, Accessibility

This is another way of thinking how to keep things at a child's-eye view. Any component of the built environment that is disproportionately scaled can make even a tall adult feel diminished. Imagine how oppressive such elements are to a child. When a community's infrastructure is outsized, it makes all residents feel insignificant. Retaining a humane scale means that building heights, parking lot footprints, signage square footage and more all stay within reasonable limits. See the Living Building Challenge for more specifics on what constitutes humane scale.

Pattern 4: Safe Crossings

Beauty, Safety, Playfulness, Joy, Accessibility

Painted cement doesn't do much to keep pedestrians out of harm's way. Develop more interactive crossing signals with sounds, colorful flags, visual pattern changes and a host of other features. This will do more to keep people engaged, entertained and protected when crossing the street.

Pattern 5: Finding Home

Safety, Playfulness, Joy, Connectedness

Identify pathways or individual neighborhoods using dedicated iconography or color palettes to help children navigate safely and independently through communities. A certain animal species' footprints could lead to schoolyards, or certain city blocks could use common front door colors. The idea is to help children find their way while making them feel celebrated instead of simply tolerated.

Pattern 6: Revealed Systems

Education, Beauty, Resilience, Playfulness, Connectedness

When we expose occupants to the systems that power their buildings, we help connect them to their built and natural surroundings. Reveal water, energy and transportation systems within structures and communities to provide living classrooms (that never close) for students of all ages. Don't hide vital operational functions; show them, study them and celebrate them so that our children can discover how to improve upon them.

Pattern 7: Tamed Commercialism

Beauty, Joy, Biophilia

Children, like all of us, deserve to walk down the street without being barraged by advertising. Cities that cater first to children and prioritize nature over marketing will limit commercial signage that barks at residents about what they should buy, do and prefer. Choosing products and services will then emerge from a more organic decision-making process based on needs instead of manufactured wants.

Pattern 8: The Child and the Seat

Beauty, Safety, Playfulness, Health, Joy, Connectedness, Biophilia, Accessibility

Since children need and want to sit with greater frequency than other people, their cities must feature a variety of seating options. Such amenities will also serve the elderly, individuals with mobility challenges and anyone who chooses walking as a primary mode of transportation. Offer seating at multiple heights, similar to the way drinking fountains and even urinals are situated in many public spaces. Seating should be located frequently on every street.

Pattern 9: Biophilia and Unstructured Play

Beauty, Playfulness, Health, Joy, Connectedness, Biophilia

Add plentiful opportunities for children and adults to interact with nature, even in the midst of urban settings. Design around fishponds, water features, fountains, climbing trees, sandboxes and anything else that allows citizens to expand on their relationships with the environment, particularly in spontaneous ways. This is one way to protect our children from what writer Richard Louv calls nature-deficit disorder. Children want to get dirty because it's fun, and it's good for them. Let's show them we approve, and then we should join them.

Pattern 10: Access to Nature

Beauty, Playfulness, Health, Joy, Connectedness, Biophilia, Accessibility

Nothing should stand between children and the natural world. Ensure that they have direct and ongoing access to non-design-based water, sunshine, trees and vistas wherever they live. Give them opportunities to visit the natural world, support their rights to nature and never let the built environment stand in the way.

Pattern 11: The Sense of Danger

Education, Resilience, Safety, Playfulness, Joy

We need to reintroduce elements of "safe danger" to our cities so our children learn how to test and master suitable boundaries. Give them balance beams, zip lines and climbing apparatis that offer them experiential knowledge of what they can and can't do. Children are better able to distinguish between real and imagined danger when they're occasionally allowed to fall.

Pattern 12: The Engineering Child

Education, Resilience, Playfulness, Connectedness

Give children opportunities to participate in their cities' changing systems so that they can observe simple cause-and-effect dynamics. Let them serve as junior hydrologists by experimenting with how a waterway alters its course when dammed. Show them the modulations in a photovoltaic array's energy draw on sunny versus rainy days. Enrich them with the option to take part in what's happening around them.

Surround children with edible landscapes so that their cities become agricultural classrooms.

Pattern 13: The Hunter/Gatherer

Education, Beauty, Resilience, Health, Joy, Biophilia

Surround children with edible landscapes so that their cities become agricultural classrooms. Start with urban farms, then extend the concept into all public spaces so that residents are able to pick and snack at any point during a stroll down the street. Plant only edible, non-toxic species, mixing fruits and berries with herbs and hardy plants that are native to the region.

Pattern 14: The Farmer

Education, Beauty, Resilience, Health, Joy, Connectedness, Biophilia

Expanding on Pattern 12, involve children in local food production efforts. Public gardens, p-patches and other resources connect people to the food they eat while also connecting them to one another and enhancing community resilience. Providing children with farming-related roles and responsibilities gives them the gift of sustainability.

Pattern 15: Decentralized Amenities

Beauty, Playfulness, Health, Joy, Connectedness, Biophilia, Accessibility

Distribute child-friendly amenities throughout a city to ensure that all citizens have ready access to them. Sprinkle bike racks, sport courts, public art, water features, revealed systems and natural playgrounds throughout the community (and not just in concentrated mega-parks). This will keep citizens of all ages healthier, happier and more likely to spend their leisure time in the outdoors rather than in front of a computer screen. If amenities are centralized its more likely that children have to be driven to use them.

Pattern 16: Amenities at the Heart

Education, Beauty, Resilience, Connectedness, Accessibility

Consider placing key community resources at the center of the community. Schools, playgrounds, gardens and other amenities offering the most advantages to the greatest portion of the population should be located in the core, with less critical services and residential structures radiating outward. This pattern stands in contrast to Pattern 15, so planners must determine the ideal approach for each community and balance between a decentralized network with key amenities that are central.

Pattern 17: Non-Toxic World

Resilience, Safety, Health

Eliminate poisonous substances from the built environment that surrounds our children. Adhere to the requirements of the Living Building Challenge's Materials Petal by using only Red List-approved supplies and substances for all community structures and infrastructure materials.

Pattern 18: Programs for Children

Education, Resilience, Joy, Connectedness

Curate activities and curriculum in schools and community centers that educate and inspire kids. These programs might be overseen by municipal parks and recreation departments and/or private non-profit organizations. Nest them with other initiatives designed to engage and support citizens of all ages as a way to bring the city's youngest and oldest citizens closer together.

Pattern 19: Universal Children's Design

Beauty, Safety, Playfulness, Joy, Connectedness, Accessibility

Expand on the concept of universal design, which caters primarily to the elderly and the physically challenged, by thinking first of how to adapt buildings and communities to children's needs. Just as universal design benefits users of all abilities, universal children's design makes things easier and more enjoyable for users of all ages.

Pattern 20: Sheltered Waiting Areas

Education, Beauty, Safety, Connectedness

Protect every generation by designing sheltered public waiting areas. Turn these structures into mini classrooms with interpretive historical information on the neighborhood, mini galleries with student art from nearby schools or mini communication centers where people can interact in writing.

Pattern 21: Public Drinking Fountains

Beauty, Safety, Playfulness, Health

Children love moving water, and everybody needs to stay hydrated. Offer this fun and healthy service throughout the city. Drinking fresh water is essential to health and reinforces appropriate hydration over drinks like soda.

Pattern 22: The Hill

Beauty, Playfulness, Health, Joy, Connectedness, Biophilia, Accessibility

Every child knows that there is something uniquely enjoyable and empowering about being on higher ground. Hills of any elevation offer endless opportunities to run, sled, roll, and take in more of the view. Reshape parks to create a modest hill in an otherwise flat region if necessary, but give people an opportunity to climb, toboggan or slide down.

Pattern 23: Swings for All Ages

Playfulness, Health, Joy, Connectedness

Swinging is intoxicating. Cities need places where everyone can experience such dizzying exhilaration, whether for stress relief, family togetherness or just for the sheer fun of it.

Pattern 24: Sound Parks

Education, Beauty, Playfulness, Joy, Biophilia

Help community members hear the music of nature by creating dedicated places where sound is celebrated and multiple senses are engaged. Imagine drums powered by fountains, wind chimes powered by the wind, or simply opportunities for musicians to regularly perform.

Pattern 25: Crazy Art

Education, Beauty, Playfulness, Joy, Connectedness

Install public art that starts by identifying place and continues by inspiring children to think beyond the ordinary. Instead of creating intersections merely with numbered roads, establish artistic navigational tools that support whimsy such as public clocks, colorful paintings and interactive sculptures.

Pattern 26: Patterned Walks

Beauty, Playfulness, Health, Joy, Connectedness

Encourage childhood games in public places for all community members. Design beautiful patterns of hopscotch squares, sidewalk skipping lines and other modules into the walkways of the city. It will invite sport, encourage rhythmic activities and allow children to lead the way.

Pattern 27: Six-Story Max

Beauty, Resilience, Safety, Health, Connectedness, Biophilia, Accessibility

Places where children live should be limited in height to six stories. This will keep residents close enough to the earth to allow them to stay connected to the natural and human elements on the ground level. Even from the roof of a six-story building, children can still see and call to their friends who pass by on the sidewalk below and make out facial features, beyond that a distinct human connection is lost. A six-story building is also walkable, children can walk the stairs to the top floors or they can scurry down to join in a street-level activity. They are never far from anything that grows in the soil. And, crucially, all buildings can be net zero living buildings.

UniverCity Development: From Living Building to Living Community

Pattern 28: House Size Mix

Beauty, Resilience, Connectedness, Accessibility

Any city celebrating children has to include a reasonable blend of house sizes and types. Plan a mix of residential structures that accommodates every resident and family grouping. Keep all larger 'family' style units as close to the ground as possible.

Pattern 29: Bedrooms to the Street

Education, Beauty, Resilience, Safety, Joy, Connectedness, Biophilia, Accessibility

Residential buildings must give children (and the adults who care for them) visual and physical access to the world outside their rooms. While this pattern is particularly important for urban apartments and multistory housing, it is important to consider in any living space. Children need a visual connection to the life of the street so that they can see people and nature in vibrant action. Design bedrooms with views of the street rather than internal courtyards.

UniverCity Development: From Living Building to Living Community

Pattern 30: Courtyards for Reflection

Education, Beauty, Resilience, Safety, Joy, Connectedness, Biophilia, Accessibility

In the hustle and bustle of the city, it's important to have places that are sanctuaries of quiet and personal reflection. Include frequent courtyards linked to public spaces that offer acoustical and visual privacy from the street.

Pattern 31: A Place for Dogs

Joy, Biophilia

Children need dogs! Create places in the city where dogs can safely run off leash. Dog parks bring communities alive. Install dog-walking infrastructure such as bag stations throughout the city and signs to keep pets on leash and safe.

Pattern 32: Small Egg Business

Education, Resilience, Joy, Biophilia

What better job than allowing children to raise chickens and collect and sell eggs? Ensure that local community bylaws allow for a small brood of chickens for each family and designate chicken spots within each development, even if on a rooftop.

In the hustle and bustle of the city, it's important to have places that are sanctuaries of quiet and personal reflection.

Pattern 33: Ground Level Fountain

Education, Beauty, Joy, Biophilia, Accessibility

Having the ability to actually run through water is a sheer delight. Fountains should be active and invite you in rather than being off-limits for play. Design public fountains that are inviting and accessible, even for wheelchairs.

Pattern 34: Neighborhood Treehouse

Joy, Biophilia, Beauty, Playfulness

Every child loves a treehouse. It encourages sociability and activity, and allows for prospect over the neighborhood. Design safe and accessible treehouses into public parks and encourage private treehouses in developments.

Pattern 35: The Wide Sidewalk

Connectedness, Safety

We've all walked along those narrow sidewalks that don't allow two people to walk side-by-side. Generous sidewalks create valuable urban space for childhood activities and games, compelling street furniture and spaces for trees. Sidewalks should be at least eight feet wide to be truly social.

Pattern 36: Bike Path Network

Connectedness, Safety, Joy, Biophilia

Nothing worries parents more than their child being hit by a car, whether crossing the street or biking on the side of the road. A bike path network separate from the automobile system encourages biking and walking, and changes the pace and enjoyment of being outside. Establish a bike network that allows people to move through a community away from automobiles for long stretches.

Pattern 37: Short Blocks and Short Cuts

Connectedness

Long city blocks diminish the quality of experience of pedestrians especially people who have short strides like children. Designing short blocks or interrupting long blocks with bisecting pedestrian pathways allows for shortcuts and reduces distances to various destinations.

Pattern 38: Clock Tower

Connectedness, Education, Safety

Having a sense of time, even if not wearing a watch, is good for children to orient themselves relative to getting home at the right hour. Perhaps more importantly, creating a local icon that helps to identify a community and provide a place to meet is essential. Meeting 'under the clock' can be a great community identifier.

Pattern 39: Community Meeting Place

Connectedness, Education, Playfulness

A children's center, community center or centralized structure where groups of children can meet for activities, birthdays and events helps to nurture a family-friendly environment. Include at least one classroom-sized building in each neighborhood that can be rented or signed out by the community. The community meeting place should have outdoor covered structures as well as an indoor climate controlled space for greater summertime use.

Pattern 40: Kid Food Vendors

Joy

Ice cream trucks, french fry vendors and other informal and mobile food concessions breathe life and periodic excitement into a neighborhood. Allow for and encourage street-side vendors to frequent neighborhood amenities and parks.

HOW TO USE THE CHILD-CENTERED PLANNING TOOL

This tool is meant to stimulate thought and reflection when designing any piece of urban fabric. It's not intended as a 'checklist', although it certainly can be used that way. It is more important to be thoughtful in how the various patterns can be used. Each community and place should feature a different mix and proportion of patterns. Intentionality is the key to child-centered planning.

Currently, the International Living Future Institute is involved in master planning the final phase of the UniverCity development at Simon Fraser University in Burnaby Mountain. Our team is using the Child-Centered Planning approach in the design in order to create a positive community for people of all ages. The plan illustrated above shows the master plan where over 1,000 units of housing are being planned as part of a mixed use urban village. Areas where we are integrating the patterns we've identified are clearly shown on the diagram. This community, that houses a childcare pursing the Living Building Challenge, will be a pioneering model of a new way to approach community design.

We surround our children with love and do everything we can to protect them from harm. But we tend to dismiss them when we plan the communities where they live, which makes no sense. It's time to nurture our cities the way we nurture our children. Following a pattern language catering to little ones will yield significant long-range benefits for everyone. Children-centered cities will be more enriching, stimulating, educational, secure, resilient and sustainable. And they will be more likely to remain thriving cities when our grandchildren–and theirs–need places to call home. ∎

> It's time to nurture our cities the way we nurture our children. Following a pattern language catering to little ones will yield significant long-range benefits for everyone. Children-centered cities will be more enriching, stimulating, educational, secure, resilient and sustainable.

THE POWER OF GOOD DESIGN

Beauty as a Force for Change

ORIGINALLY PUBLISHED 2014

"Beauty awakens the soul to act."

Dante

For a long time it seemed like "good design" was the exclusive providence of European or Japanese designers — especially around products and the everyday things in our lives. In North America, it always felt like we put quantity over quality and size over substance. Our cars, clothing, furniture, consumer goods and even architecture were always considered better in Italy, Scandinavia, France, Spain or the UK. Americans had more "stuff," but our stuff's designs seemed cheap and poorly considered, especially as we outsourced the actual manufacturing to faraway places.

I became even more convinced of this as I began to study design in its various contexts — as applied architecture and the design of neighborhoods and cities. Just look at the transformation of our urban and suburban environments between the 1960s–1990s. When we redesigned everything for the automobile, we threw out every good design principle — places of beauty became the exception, and entire communities in North America often lacked a single beautiful place that hadn't been created prior to World War II.

The more I thought about it, the more I realized that the countries that were producing such beautiful things enjoyed a *culture of design*. Rather than prioritizing size and quantity, as we North Americans did (and still do, although to a mercifully lesser extent), these foreign cultures valued beauty and quality; design was something that was discussed and appreciated by the greater population. People in these places were sophisticated enough to understand the importance of craft and good design, whereas we abandoned this culture in our all-encompassing adoption of mass consumer culture. It was the difference between a philosophical shift as a nation of "consumers" versus "citizens" who sometimes consumed things. The difference was evident when even mass-produced items

coming from such regions were given better design consideration. Think about the revolution that was IKEA, with the Swedes showing us that even mass-produced, inexpensive items should be well designed. IKEA understood that people deserve to be surrounded by things that show manufacturers care for them.

The thing I find very interesting right now is that all of this appears to be shifting — both here in the United States and Canada, and more generally around the world. A new culture of design is emerging, and it has great potential, especially because it's sometimes paired up with social justice and sustainability. The convergence of these three issues provides incredible promise for change. Beauty, social justice and sustainability are three critical legs of a stool to reimagine the future of all of humanity's artifacts. Of these, beauty has become the key fulcrum for change — when you appeal to people's desires, you have the potential to break down barriers that were keeping them from embracing the critical issues of how design impacts people and the planet.

Beauty becomes the key fulcrum for change — when you appeal to people's desires, you have the potential to break down barriers that were keeping them from embracing the critical issues of how design impacts people and the planet.

EARLY AESTHETIC BARRIERS TO GREEN BUILDING

We have watched a similar pattern play out with the green design movement from the late sixties up until today. In the early days of the movement, "green" buildings were lauded for their environmentally friendly, energy-conserving performance, but were often seen as ugly, uncomfortable and impractical. The lack of beauty in many of the pioneering green projects actually set the movement back at least two decades — people equated green design with bad design. Let's face it: Few sustainable structures built between the 1970s and the early 2000s would have won any beauty contests. They were undeniably innovative and broke important ground that ultimately benefited the movement, but they were perceived as unattractive, and a schism grew between those who practiced green design and those who practiced good design.[1] For a long time, green clients were few and far between because people did not want an ungainly green building. As a result, many people who now embrace sustainable design waited to do so because they thought green buildings failed to offer form, function and favorability.

Trying to sell people on green design back then was a lot like pushing castor oil: People knew it was beneficial but just couldn't stomach the idea, or the bad taste. The diehards would do it, but the taste was just too bad for the masses to adopt it. Architects felt that sustainability would interfere with their craft, while project owners hesitated to gamble on what were considered experimental approaches.

Still, the green design movement moved forward, thanks to the relentless work of pioneers who understood what was at stake. Slowly, design and quality began to merge with performance and responsibility.[2]

---

1 This schism has also persisted in schools of design and architecture.

2 It's important to emphasize that this period of engineering and systems-oriented innovation was integral to the movement's ability to advance. We stand on the shoulders of the men and women who pioneered these ideas, and we would not be where we are today without their contributions.

THE APPLE REVOLUTION

I was an early fan of Apple® because they were one of the few American companies founded on the premise that design really does matter. Even as I tracked the company's ups and downs in the marketplace during the 1990s, I always felt confident that they would persevere. In fact, I was adamant that the Apple way would one day dominate the market. I admired how they prioritized the way consumers would *feel* while using their products. Instead of focusing exclusively on what their stuff did, they thought about *why* people would buy and *how* the product could change the customer experience forever. Apple was among the first manufacturers to consider experience alongside performance. Everything from the font designs to the ergonomics was carefully thought through, and only the beautiful options made the final cut.[3]

Apple is successful because beauty and experience are carefully integrated into their products, wrapping existing technologies in well-designed packages. I don't believe it's an exaggeration to credit Apple with planting the seeds of a culture of design that was previously lacking in North America — it's remarkable what Jobs, Ive[4] and others in Apple did to reinvent music, computers, animation and telecommunications.

Having said this, I am not a total Apple "fanboy" — design alone is not success — and Apple received considerable (and deserved) criticism for the lack of environmental and social progress they were making in their overseas factories. Apple still has work to do in order to demonstrate that all three issues (beauty, social and environmental responsibility) are at the core of their business, and the company could take a page from Gates on philanthropy.

ARCHITECTURE GETS ON BOARD

Just as Apple helped shift public opinion about the importance of beauty in manufactured goods, we are now seeing a dramatic shift in people's insistence on beauty in the green building movement. Green buildings are, dare I say it, getting sexy. Over the last decade in particular, beautiful, deep green projects have emerged. Their designs are beginning to embody a depth and meaning that ultimately gives them greater value in financial, environmental and emotional terms.

---

3   When I came to Cascadia in 2006, one of my first executive acts was to convert the office computers from PCs to Macs. This idea was met with more than a little resistance, particularly from those who said the existing system worked just fine. But I felt strongly then, as I still do today, that our organization needs to reflect our core principles: first, that we must project success in order to achieve success and secondly, that beauty and performance can exist in harmony. We donated our PCs, shifted to a Mac environment and then watched with interest as the iPhone came out the next year.

4   John Ive is the head of design for Apple and the creative force behind Apple's amazing products.

The simple yet beautiful SFU Childcare Center — a Living Building project. Photo: Martin Tessler

We have LEED to thank in part for pushing this trend. As the standard began to build steam, it brought many new projects into the fold — many of these competing for design excellence as well as LEED points. More clients expressed interest in green elements, which pulled more designers onto the projects. Suddenly, sustainable projects were winning design awards and the days of "green is ugly and weird" as a construct were coming to an end. It was the Living Building Challenge (in my biased opinion) that tipped the issue completely.

The Living Building Challenge was the first standard to include a Beauty requirement; here is a program that sets the highest bar in the world for environmental performance, yet insists that good design and aesthetics meet or exceed the quality of the world's best architecture. This simple step (which was so obvious in hindsight) was a bit of a revolution, as it emphasized the experiential as on par with the performance metric — neither dominating, but both important to success. Initially, this generated a great deal of discussion. Skeptics argued that such a subjective, unquantifiable thing shouldn't be included alongside measurable aspects like energy and water performance, and that this would diminish the seriousness of the program. We insisted that this aspect of the Challenge was arguably one of its most critical, as no Living Building can succeed unless it offers and inspires beauty. Our obligation is to create a better world — if Living Buildings were ugly, we wouldn't be successful.

In fact, these structures should be more beautiful than others of the built environment, because they are imbued with more meaning. Ironically, it is the Beauty petal that has probably inspired more people to take up the challenge than any single program element.

Now that stunning Living Buildings are blooming all around the world, the one-time skeptics have come around to our way of thinking. A responsibly built environment, they now see, depends fully on its beauty. One of the most rewarding things we've witnessed is how this focus has challenged the thinking of even left-brained individuals. When you have engineers asking "How can I make my mechanical system beautiful?" you know you are on to something special.

THE PRODUCTS REVOLUTION

Building on what Apple has started, there has been a huge shift in the consumer product market. This shift has begun to change the consumer experience, and consumer expectations are now rising. It's no longer enough to compete with price and options. People now expect their products to change experience. As these expectations continue to rise, it is time to further inject corporate social and environmental responsibility into the experience. Here are a few examples of the new thinking that is emerging:

NEST. Who could have predicted that people would clamor to buy a thermostat, or go to an Apple Store to purchase one? The idea that a thermostat could be sexy and change behavior was groundbreaking. NEST is powerful because it makes something that is ubiquitous in all our buildings beautiful and fun to use, whereas other thermostats are ugly and daunting to use. The net benefit is that people save considerable energy with such a small investment, and more importantly, they begin to change their relationship with energy. The thermostat and the user begin to learn together. Imagine 20-30 percent energy reductions simply through a simple interface? NEST is on a roll now with their new smoke detector — changing the paradigm and experience that will literally save lives.

Dyson. Here, too, is a company that redefined their niche through design. Fed up with the paradigm of ugly, poorly performing and messy-to-clean vacuums, they didn't tinker — they redefined. The Dyson vacuum has been instrumental in changing the consumer mindset around what was acceptable around a product. They continue to branch out and are redefining the hand-drying experience and special faucets that incorporate the drying unit into the faucet itself — eliminating mess. They think about common consumer challenges and present solutions that are more effective, often more energy efficient, and always more beautiful. Like all the products I mention here, Dyson's products are category definers — influencing every other company in their sector to think differently.

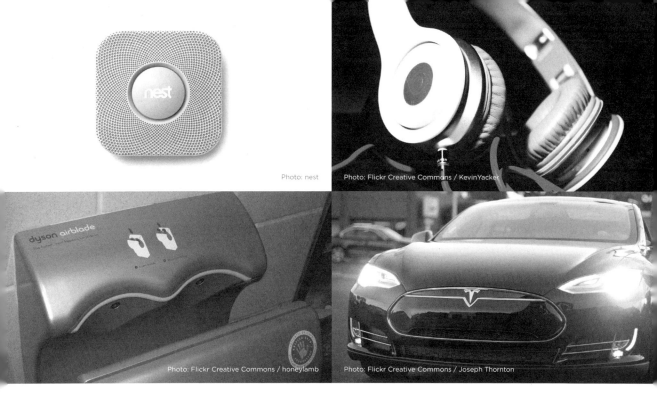

Photo: nest
Photo: Flickr Creative Commons / KevinYacker
Photo: Flickr Creative Commons / honeylamb
Photo: Flickr Creative Commons / Joseph Thornton

The new paradigm of products that reinvent the experience of using everyday objects.

Beats. Dr. Dre and his product designers put the 'cool' back in over-the-head headphones with the introduction of Beats in 2008. While plenty of competitive products now offer a comparable listening experience, Beats fly off the shelves for hundreds of dollars because they changed the story and design factor around their products. As far as I know, Beats has not yet embraced the other two legs of the stool, but they represent the kind of thinking about form and function that is a good starting point.

Tesla. I've written previously about how much I admire this company and its innovations. They took an idea that always had promise — the electric car — and infused it with bleeding-edge technology to reimagine the product category. Early generations of electric cars suffered from mechanical issues, poor range and mediocre performance profiles. Electric cars used to be like taking the castor oil. Tesla changed all of that with a paradigm-shifting alternative that can take you from Boston to LA with free recharges along the way — all while looking drop-dead gorgeous. As the company moves into more affordable production vehicles, it has the potential to change everything about the automotive industry. Imagine the end of gas stations and the polluting, corrupt pipeline behind it? Tesla can.

It's time to reinvent many simple building materials as I did with the Earth Measure reclaimed stone product line.

Ecovative Design. This company has proven that anything can be wrapped in beauty. Ecovative's young founders came up with a way to grow organic mushroom mycelium and combine it with agricultural waste to create packaging, insulation and consumer products that are environmentally restorative. Their "Mushroom Materials" have the potential to rid the world of plastic packaging.[5] What could be more beautiful than that? I was pleased to serve on the jury of the 2013 Buckminster Fuller Prize that they won. The potential here is vast — imagine if it was a good thing to throw something away; imagine if our waste could build soil and return nutrients; imagine if our packaging was completely non-toxic and edible.

Earth Measure. Sometimes you have to rethink age-old building materials and recognize their inherent sustainability. Natural stone is one of the greenest products currently available, but for some reason it has been overlooked by the green building industry. Earth Measure (who just won a Top Ten Green Product award from Building Green) could change all that by turning the waste stream of the stone industry into a cladding and paving product instead of down-grading it. This product offers great promise and higher value, and it captures the embodied energy that has already been expended to serve as a durable product for the next few

---

5   Ecovative Design was a 2013 winner of the Buckminster Fuller Challenge.

hundred years. It has been my pleasure to work with ColdSpring on this new product line, which takes what was once discarded and converts it into a useable material with patterns inspired by the natural world.

THE NEW PARADIGM

Elevating good design is about creating a new normal for a new generation. As a society, we need to elevate our expectations. Everything we make has an impact on people and on the planet; it's our responsibility to ensure that we carefully consider all of these impacts and only produce things that are worthwhile. Producing products and buildings we love and care for helps create a framework for extending our expectations outward to the impacts to people and the environment. It would be unfortunate if this new culture of design only led to buying more stuff. I am optimistic, as I believe this new culture is changing how people look at and evaluate the things around them — to ask more deep questions — to ask "Do I need this? Will this enrich my life?" The results of thinking differently can be profound.

As beauty becomes commonplace, the consuming public (including building owners and developers) will come to expect nothing less. We're even seeing the sexification of energy — photovoltaic panels that once aroused ardent NIMBYism are now incorporated into the aesthetic strategies of many structures.

New companies are redefining their products in ways that make things that people once ignored into important components of their lives — and along the way are saving energy and resources.

> **Good design, in all its forms, will win out.**

Soon, when it comes to our buildings, our communities, and all the things we fill them with, the ugly, polluting and unjust simply won't be tolerated. By proving that we can simultaneously achieve good design and good environmental performance, we are changing the status quo. People will no longer blithely accept that cities should be broken up by interstates; that skyscrapers should climb so high that occupants lose all connection to nature; that nuclear power plants should dot the rural landscape.

Good design, in all its forms, will win out.

To elevate the value of beauty, we must pursue it in everything we design, everything we use, and everything we build — beginning with the most basic ingredients we choose, and extending outward into the largest cities we plan. As humans, we are wired to crave beauty. As citizens of the planet, we are responsible for surrounding one another with built and manufactured environments that elicit emotional connections. Beauty is the tie that binds; ugliness is incompatible with a restorative world. ∎

———————————————

SALVAGE MODERNISM

A New Design Philosophy, Aesthetic and Ecological Approach

ORIGINALLY PUBLISHED 2015

It goes against the principles of Salvage Modernism to deliberately steal, pilfer or prematurely undermine an existing or historic structure in order to extract salvage materials.

I have never much liked buildings that pretend to be old by mimicking building styles from the past, like all the fake neocolonial and "Tudor" buildings that can be found everywhere. I guess that makes me a modernist. My belief is that all buildings should reflect the age in which they were built, and modern buildings should be true to the ways in which they are built today.

But when I look at old building materials I always get excited — the history, patina and frankly quality of materials from decades ago is often far superior to what we can find today. Every year, thousands of buildings are taken down, and hundreds of thousands of tons of still useful material is simply landfilled, a huge and disappointing waste of resources. Thankfully, there is also a growing economy of architectural salvage places with significant gems available (items are sometimes overpriced, but often good deals abound.) The key is having time to look and the means to act quickly and then to stockpile the good materials you find — and then knowing how best to integrate them into your design for maximum effect. A balance has to be struck so that materials of vastly different age don't create a disharmonious whole.

Over a decade ago I began experimenting with what I coined "salvage modernism," which is the integration of salvaged materials into modern construction such that the beauty of the salvaged object is displayed and honored. In the early 2000s, my good friend Chris DeVolder and I began to design a net zero house and barn for an organic farmer in Weston, Missouri, called Green Dirt Farm. We wanted to push the heavy use of salvaged materials, and our client was very much on board with that approach. Over the next year, we shopped around for salvage materials of all types and collected a highly interesting group of materials ranging from wood, doors, hardware, lights, stained glass, terra cotta and more. With this special palette at our disposal, we began to design the buildings, which required using unique and often irregular items and thus meant some really careful detailing and planning. The project was likely one of the first to use eBay as a source of building materials, as we spent a great deal of time looking for just the right pieces in this burgeoning e-commerce hub that had just gone public and was only beginning to scale.

Our design for the Green Dirt Farm received considerable attention locally and nationally — being featured on the cover of Jennifer Roberts' 2005 book, *Redux: Designs that Reveal, Recycle and Redefine*, which focused on using salvage materials. The house also won several local design awards, showing that salvage materials can increase the beauty of a project.

After the successful completion of the project, I began to think through the principles that had emerged for me, particularly one that takes this idea to the level of a simple but elegant new design philosophy.

THE SALVAGE MODERNISM PHILOSOPHY

The philosophy of Salvage Modernism is one where a designer seeks to integrate substantial amounts of reused/salvaged materials as both artifact and replacement for modern materials, embedded within an otherwise modern architectural design, and using modern construction methods. What makes it modern? A true expression of materials, honestly utilized through modern construction techniques. What is salvage? Any material that was used previously on another project or for another use prior to re-use.

The purpose of Salvage Modernism is decidedly not to make a building look "old" (although it can make it hard to date the building, which is fine) or to mimic historical styles, but to offer up, display and honor materials that deserve a second life within the context of a modern design. Doing so does in fact help a project feel timeless, but in an authentic way. A fake expression of materials goes against the grain of this philosophy and is replaced with the simple acknowledgement that there is inherent beauty in materials that have aged and seen prior use.

> **Salvage Modernism**
> The artful integration of salvaged architectural artifacts in abundance, into modern design.

A principle tenet of this philosophy is that a new project is enhanced precisely because of the juxtaposition of the old and the new. New materials used alongside salvaged artifacts therefore should not be artificially aged or made to match the salvage materials in appearance, especially if the methods of making the materials have changed since the original period. The purpose is not to use materials to make an old design aesthetic, but rather to include the old materials within a modern aesthetic.

There's a big difference.

It goes against the principles of Salvage Modernism to deliberately steal, pilfer or prematurely undermine an existing or historic structure in order to extract salvage materials. Historic buildings deserve to be saved and preserved in their entirety as part of the cultural heritage of our communities. Salvaged materials should therefore be found honestly — when a building's life is truly over, or as materials are discarded because of remodeling or damage.

It is also important to reuse salvaged materials from projects within a reasonable distance so as not to increase the embodied carbon of using the materials through transportation impacts. Deliberately importing salvaged materials from across the globe is inappropriate and wasteful,

PRINCIPLES OF SALVAGE MODERNISM

1. Salvaged materials must be used in enough abundance to be visible in most major spaces in a structure without creating a disharmonious whole.

2. Salvaged Modernism projects are prohibited from including irresponsible salvage through prematurely damaging or dismantling historic structures.

3. Salvaged materials may not be used to produce an artificial or misleading historic aesthetic that makes the overall project seem old or built in a previous era and historic style.

4. Salvaged materials should be sourced from as close at hand as possible, preferably following the Living Building Challenge sourcing requirements.

5. Salvaged materials must be integrated into new construction using modern construction materials and methods wherever possible.

6. Modern materials can't be aged to match or to blur distinction between old and new. The juxtaposition between old and new is critical to the philosophy.

7. Salvaged materials can be used to introduce delight, whimsy, mystery, timelessness, art and history into a modern building — in direct opposition to traditional modernist dogma that says to remove all ornamentation. In this philosophy, the ornamentation is the salvaged items themselves.

8. Salvaged materials can be used in non-traditional ways or ways that differ from their original intended use (in fact, that's encouraged).

Over a decade ago I began experimenting with what I coined "salvage modernism," which is the integration of salvaged materials into modern construction such that the beauty of the salvaged object is displayed and honored.

although using materials from afar is of course appropriate if they were taken out of local existing buildings.

As a result of using local salvage in lieu of new materials, a reduction in embodied energy and resource impacts is inherent in the Salvage Modernism approach. Finding ways to use materials that have served in buildings for years, decades or perhaps centuries, instead of new ones that

Salvaged stained glass windows at Green Dirt Farm in Weston, Missouri

Nighttime rendering of Heron Hall entry showing salvaged door

have to be mined, extracted or manufactured is a great thing because the carbon and other impacts have already been expended.

The philosophy of Salvage Modernism requires sufficient quantities of salvaged material integration in order to truly be named as such. A single salvaged artifact does not make a project a Salvage Modernist project. It is my belief that the salvaged materials should in fact have a visible presence through the majority of spaces and facades of a structure so as to make a meaningful contribution to the environmental footprint reduction and to bring a sense of timelessness and cultural story to the entirety of a project. How much is enough to warrant the term? That should always be a matter of debate, but the amount of salvage should be noticeable throughout the project.

HERON HALL

When it was time to design and build my own house, I knew I wanted to revisit this philosophy and take it to the next level. I decided to call the house Heron Hall (as a dedication to the herons that live nearby). After I secured the property for the project, I began searching for two years for unique and beautiful materials in which to design with. Luckily in Seattle I had access to two incredible architectural salvage places — Earthwise

STARTING YOUR SALVAGE MODERNISM PROJECT

Designing a project using the Salvage Modernism philosophy is rewarding, and the outcome can be profound. As you consider your project keep these few tips in mind:

Collect early: it can take time to find the right pieces — expect many months of searching before you begin designing — and keep searching as you design.

Budget wisely: If you're lucky, you can save greatly on materials for your project and certainly will have better quality material for your dollar, but keep in mind that a lot of salvaged materials take considerable labor to fix, refinish and integrate than new materials, so those savings can easily vanish, and additional costs might even accrue.

Enjoy the story: It's a rewarding experience to uncover the hidden stories in the materials we find — ultimately it creates projects with more character and nuance.

Don't overdo it: be careful not to turn your project into a junkyard (unless you're going for that). Too many salvage materials can overpower a space, especially if the artifacts clash aesthetically. As with any design philosophy, skill matters, and engaging a talented architect and interior designer will help you find the most elegant ways to work with salvage.

Get to know your source: People in the salvage business can be immensely helpful — keeping an eye out for materials as they come in — and giving you creative ideas. Find the best local salvage yards in your area and spend time there and talk to the employees! Also, don't forget on-line vendors like Etsy and eBay.

Be decisive: It can be heartbreaking to hesitate and lose out on some great material before you can act. Since salvage materials tend to be one of a kind, once someone buys it, it's gone. Many salvage places allow you to put temporary holds on material to give you time to make your decision and check if it will work. Still, be prepared to buy things when you see them.

> As a result of using local salvage in lieu of new materials, a reduction in embodied energy and resource impacts is inherent in the Salvage Modernism approach.

Salvage and Second Use Salvage. Many communities also have Habitat For Humanity Restores, which stockpile used and salvage materials. I also began to use Etsy as a wonderful place to search for handcrafted materials from local artisans who were repurposing old materials.

During this time I stumbled upon some real finds, including incredible materials that had been imported many years ago and then discarded. A few examples of what's going into the house:

- Giant stained glass windows from a 1920s Seattle church. The stained glass originally came from Europe, was assembled as window units by Povey brothers in Portland at the turn of the last century and then lived for eighty years in the church. Another 100 years in Heron Hall is next!

- Carved stone Foo dogs, originally from Indonesia and brought over to Seattle area for a local residence where they resided for many years before being discarded — and finally guarding the entrance to Heron Hall in a whimsical manner.

- Beautiful hand carved doors from Afghanistan, also originally brought over for another project in Seattle a decade ago and then discarded. These will be integrated into the entryway as well as the master closet.

- All the interior doors — every single one — selected from salvage yards in Seattle. Most of the doors were built between 1910 and 1940.

- Several interior stained glass and divided lite windows, including a couple of large ones that will provide daylight into the unconditioned bike barn. The poor energy performance means they can't be used thermally, but as interior windows or in unconditioned spaces, they are great.

- An old clawfoot bathtub... beautiful!

Rendering for staircase on Heron Hall, a Living Building Challenge Registered Project

Carved stone Foo Dogs at Heron Hall

Salvaged Terra Cotta

214 TRANSFORMATIONAL THOUGHT II

When it was time to design and build my own house, I knew I wanted to revisit this philosophy and take it to the next level. I decided to call the house Heron Hall (as a dedication to the herons that live nearby). After I secured the property for the project, I began searching for two years for unique and beautiful materials in which to design with.

- 100-year-old, beat-up tin ceiling, to be restored for a bathroom.
- Tons of salvage wood for interior paneling — including an old redwood wine vat that will become siding, end block slices from waste wood as paneling, and lots of salvage flooring from the region!
- Old light fixtures that will be refitted with LED bulbs.
- Old bee skeps (wicker beehives) repurposed as light fixtures.

And this is just some of what is in store.

The list is quite extensive and makes up a sizeable portion of the house's bill of materials, greatly reducing the embodied energy and ecological footprint of Heron Hall. Since the project is also a registered Living Building Challenge project, the use of salvaged materials also greatly simplifies the Materials Petal requirements of the project. ■

THE HABITAT OF HUMANITY

A Wild to Clinical Continuum

ORIGINALLY PUBLISHED 2015

What are the biologic implications of transitioning a species that evolved under the stars for over two million years to rarely ever seeing a star?

Every generation has a tendency to consider its way of living to be normal — the way it always was, how it will continue and how it should be. We are self-centered that way, which makes some sense because our patterns of behavior make up our entire direct context. History lessons sometimes seem abstract, and the future hasn't happened yet. We know that things have changed greatly in the last few centuries — especially in the last several decades with regards to our environment. This is particularly true when we consider the human habitat — the environment we have created to provide ourselves with security and shelter.

In the span of just a handful of generations, we humans have radically altered our surroundings. We've transitioned out of the natural habitat where we spent our first 200,000 years and hurled ourselves into one that is increasingly artificial, and there's no way that the pace of natural human evolution can keep up with the environmental changes we've created. In our relentless march forward, we haven't stopped long enough to consider how the radical change in our homes, offices and cities are affecting us. It's time for us to ask what short- and long-term effects our new habitat is imposing on our species and the environment.

Photo: Unsplash / Nicolai Berntsen

FROM OUTSIDE TO INSIDE

Think about the vast difference between how people live in the industrialized world today versus where the majority of their ancestors dwelled; "creature comforts" are almost exclusively focused on the interior of buildings and homes, while not-so-distant predecessors lived the majority of life outside. This is a simple observation loaded with profound implications. What are the biological implications of transitioning a species that evolved under the stars for over two million years to one that rarely ever sees a star?

Places such as Shanghai, Tokyo and Mexico City offer extreme examples of densely urbanized megacities, human communities that have literally become unnatural in an alarmingly short period of time, with more concrete than trees. Too many people are crowded into overbuilt, artificial landscapes that have cropped up in just the past two centuries with the majority of the population growth happening since 1945.[1] Modern-day humans in these habitats have too few opportunities to interact with the natural environment as they go about their days; many children never

---

1 www.nae.edu/Publications/Bridge/UrbanizationEngineering/MegacitiesandtheDevelopingWorld.aspx

As with anything, there is an ideal balance — a place where things are in harmony and optimal conditions are achieved; a sweet spot between the pre-industrial past and over-industrialized present; an internal "Boundary of Disconnect" that we cross at our peril.

have the opportunity to climb a tree or experience true, untouched nature. With light pollution, dark skies are a thing of the past.

Will this rapid variation in human habitat unleash rapid evolutionary change, and is that change already underway? Will we experience a type of punctuated equilibrium similar to the sudden modifications seen in species that are abruptly isolated by natural phenomena? Will the humans of tomorrow begin to develop different attributes in response to a separation from the natural world? Will our new manufactured environments weaken us in some critical way?

We'll begin with the understanding that modern humans are at least 200,000 years old; however, given the drastic changes introduced by industrialization and technology, it is not an exaggeration to say that our species created wholesale changes to our environment only within the last 100 years, or 1/2000 of our history — a mere blip. Factoring in archaic humans (that share 99 percent of our DNA) dating back two million years, our "new habitat" represents only 1/20,000 of our current environmental context.

For several million years, our humanoid ancestors lived almost completely outdoors, using only caves, trees and crude shelters for respite from the elements. Humans rose with the sun and slept when it was dark. They were guided by moonlight and starlight and, later, by firelight. They breathed pristine air that was free of chemicals (except perhaps in caves with fire). They drank only water and ate an omnivore's diet of nuts, grubs, vegetables, fruit, meat and fish. The normal routine provided constant exercise, since following the herds and moving with the seasons meant that everyone walked an estimated average of five to nine miles each day.[2] There were short periods of intense stress (adrenaline flowed when large carnivores were approaching, for example) and longer periods of idle time as hunter-gatherers, likely without the chronic long-term stress that we know today. They stood, squatted or sat on hard objects

2 thepaleodiet.com/run-hunt-workouts-compare/#.VmDDP2SrRGF

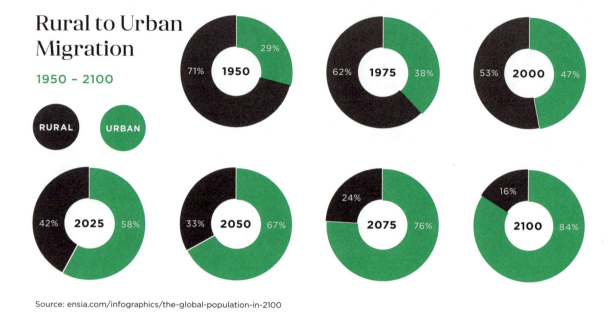

Source: ensia.com/infographics/the-global-population-in-2100

for much of the time,³ and ate dirt and bugs while coexisting intimately with other organisms — that sometimes tormented them and sometimes shaped how long they lived in a particular place.⁴ They adapted to varying degrees of temperature fluctuations, and relied on all five of the senses for survival. I could go on, but the picture is clear.

Now consider current conditions for affluent humans in the developed world — most people in this segment spend about 90 percent of their time indoors.⁵ They breathe air that contains a veritable soup of chemicals and pollutants (especially in crowded cities), and those who are smokers intentionally inhale approximately 7,000 toxic chemicals. During those hours indoors, where the temperature is often set at a constantly comfortable 72 degrees Fahrenheit, they typically sit in chairs or lie in beds — few stand for long periods anymore. There is habituated sedation, which led to a lack of sufficient exercise and an obesity epidemic.

Their diets don't serve them well either. Most people in industrialized nations consume copious quantities of foods that are high in sugar, fat and salt. They ingest an overabundance of calories and multiple chemical pre-

---

3   It is fair to say that we evolved being slightly uncomfortable to very uncomfortable nearly all the time.
4   Humans would often move dwelling units as soon as pests became too numerous in any location.
5   greenguard.org/en/consumers/consumers_iaq.aspx

servatives with every meal. They drink far too little water, usually replacing it with beverages laden again with chemicals, sugar and often alcohol.

On average, they do not get enough natural light during the day but instead bathe themselves in too much artificial light at night — something researchers are finding is terrible for the circadian system that regulates the digestive and immune systems. Their bodies and indoor environments are sterilized, destroying the beneficial microbial communities that have evolved with the species. Many work and live in a state of constant background stress due to the pace of life and the work environment. And they stare at computer screens for hours (which is hardly natural), but spend only minutes looking at trees and other life beyond their pets.

The developed world has unconsciously dotted the built landscape with natural placeholders to sate a missing desire: hanging images of nature on interior walls; building parks into cities' plans; caging animals in zoos to observe them from a safe distance. In so doing, we have trapped ourselves in a cage of our own making. All of these attempts to surround ourselves with stand-ins for the natural world stem from a collective sense of loss.

The urban living trend is driving the new normal for human habitats, and unleashing a grand experiment on the human condition. What happens when you completely change the environment of the majority of a species? Many modern cities do not provide humans with the elements necessary to thrive in the natural manner with which they evolved, yet migration to urban dwellings is rapidly increasing.[6] While approximately half of the global population lives in cities today, a much larger percentage of humans will flock to urban areas by the turn of the next century. This urbanization of our habitat becomes an experiment on a majority of our kind. It is important to note that even our "rural" environments bear little resemblance to the way humans used to live.

WHEN EVERYTHING WE WANT IS THE OPPOSITE OF WHAT WE NEED

I want to be very clear that I don't pine for the "way things were" or romanticize our hunter-gatherer past. Pre-modern life was not always idyllic, and current ways of life are not always apocalyptic. On the contrary, life for our ancestors was short and brutish. Technological advancements in the developed world have delivered some undeniable benefits to humanity. It's hard to deny progress on so many fronts, but there needs to be a limit, beyond which too much separation begins to lead us down a path of regression. I'm afraid we've passed that point.

---

[6] 2015 marks the approximate year that the majority of the world's population will live in cities. instead of rural conditions. Currently, 50% of humanity now lives in urbanized communities.

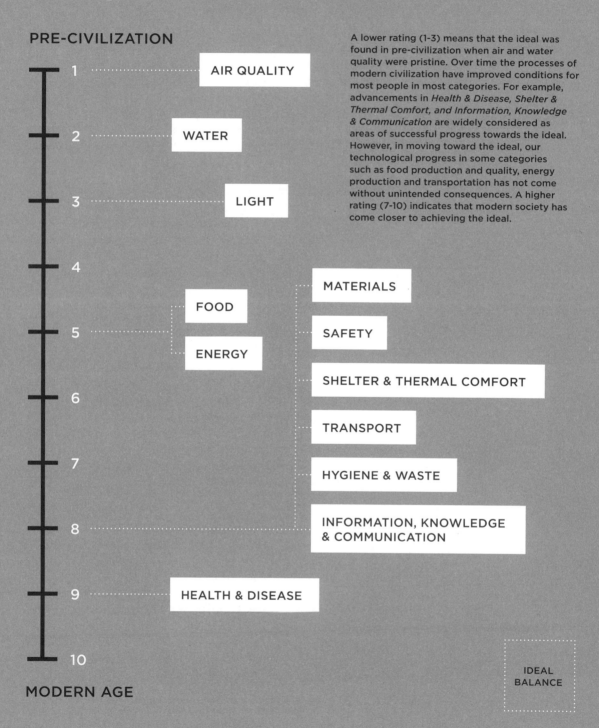

AIR QUALITY

Past: Air was once pristine, uncontaminated by human-made chemicals and pollutants, although pollens, airborne particles and fires diminished local air quality from time to time.

Present: Chemicals, auto exhaust, smoke and particulates choke the air around the world. Our lungs have not evolved to be resilient to particles of certain sizes.

Suggested Ideal: Clean air should be available everywhere — in, around and beyond even our busiest and most productive cities. Clearly, we have slid backwards relative to the air we breathe in substantial ways. The past was the ideal for air quality, with the exception of fires within caves or confined areas.

RATING: 1

WATER

Past: Water was derived from lakes, rivers, wells and springs. Water for the most part was pure, clean and in much of the world, abundant.

Present: The developed world pipes and pumps water throughout cities and towns, heavily treat it due to pollutants, chemicals, prescription drugs and impacts directly from agriculture, industry and automobiles.

Suggested Ideal: We need the predictability of clean water that is free of chemicals, hormones, pharmaceuticals and other pollutants. In the built environment, we have the technology and the experience to use net zero (or even net positive) water strategies in every structure and to rely primarily on rainwater that is distilled and naturally cleaner. Knowing what we know, we can test water more frequently and treat with UV and other filtration techniques without the use of chemicals.

RATING: 2

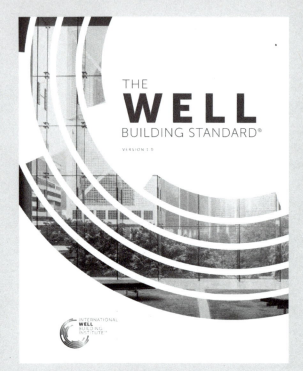

LIGHT

Present: Candles, streetlights and municipal electrical grids gradually allowed us to shine light on virtually any corner of our communities, both indoors and outdoors. Artificial lighting and light cycles that ignore our natural circadian rhythm have become the norm. In general people now live with too little light during the day — and too much light at night, upsetting our circadian systems. The counterpoint is of course that the access to light on our terms greatly enhanced our economic productivity and creativity and ability to get done what needed to get done.

Suggested Ideal: There is scientific evidence that light plays a significant role in our physical and emotional wellness. Specifically, the hypothalamic SCN, which is the master circadian pacemaker in mammals and drives diurnal rhythms in behavior, physiology, endocrinology and metabolism, is directly affected by light. The ideal human habitat would feature circadian-supportive lighting systems and much less light at night, with people sleeping in truly dark conditions and significantly less access to electronically generated light at night. Again, spending more time outside would greatly benefit us.

Much of what I have learned about the health implications of light comes from the work I have done with The WELL Building Standard®, the world's first building standard that prioritizes human health and wellness. Light is one of the Standard's seven performance categories, and structures aspiring to WELL Certification must meet certain targets to help maximize the advantageous properties of natural light for the benefit of occupants and visitors. More information about the WELL Building Standard is available at delos.com/about/well-building-standard.

RATING: 3

FOOD

Past: Hunters and gatherers had access to all of nature's bounty that was within regional reach. Diets were obviously organic and local, although there were often nutritional deficiencies to contend with, and starvation was a real possibility. Spoiled food and food-borne illness were often a reality.

Present: The modern diet in the developed world has become mechanized and overly chemical laden at the same time that it has also become generally safer. Consumers use convenience and price to justify the demand for packaged, modified foods. Too many calories from an overabundance of sugar, fat and salt make up our diets.

Suggested Ideal: We need organic, balanced diets that offer an abundance of nutrition and flavor while supporting our physical health. Significantly less fat, sugar and salt and processed foods and dairy with less meat consumption is the ideal. The ideal is likely somewhere between where we've come from and where we are today.

RATING: 5

ENERGY

Past: There was a time when humans relied only on the sun, fire, wind and moving water to deliver power.

Present: Today, we turn to coal, fossil fuels and nuclear technologies for most of our energy, with disastrous consequences.

Suggested Ideal: It's time to return to the fundamentals while harnessing our innovations. Renewable energy sources, while on the rise, must once again become our primary means of power. The time of dangerous, polluting forms of energy must come to an end.

RATING: 5

MATERIALS

Past: We once built only from place, using supplies and materials that could be harvested locally. There were no embedded chemicals, no toxic formulations, and no shipments of goods from across the globe.

Present: Too many goods and supplies contain harmful toxic ingredients that threaten the immediate health of the human species and the long-term health of the planet. Many materials that are used to build habitats are imported from far away — requiring copious energy to ship and discounting the value of regional assets. The extraction of materials has had a significant negative impact on the environment.

Suggested Ideal: Buildings and communities — along with the products that fill them — must be constructed from healthy, locally sourced, non-toxic materials. We must learn from nature and create materials with the same processes the natural world uses (biomimicry), use materials longer, and ensure closed-loop cycles for some durable materials and biodegradable nutrient cycles for others.

RATING: 8

SAFETY

Past: Humans used to be a great food source for many predators. Internal warfare and strife also plagued our entire history. Natural formations (caves, trees and hills) were used for protection and we began to develop arms and to build more defensible structures for safety.

Present: Humans have killed nearly all natural predators, and our life expectancies have increased dramatically. While war and strife afflict much of humanity, it can be argued that we are safer than humans were in the past. Today, fellow humans are more of a threat than predatory animals are, but due to the potential destructive powers of weapons and climate change, safety and security is on the decline.

Suggested Ideal: Clearly we need to soften our violent tendencies, improve cross-cultural human relations, and eliminate poverty in order to improve our overall safety, particularly in urban settings. The world needs to significantly de-escalate arms and make a global commitment to fighting the climate change and habitat and species loss that threaten long-term security.

RATING: 8

SHELTER & THERMAL COMFORT

Past: We were climate-dependent, and lived within diurnal and seasonal temperature shifts. We were often hot or cold, and many people died due to heat exhaustion or hypothermia. The discovery of fire was one of the first solutions in our timeless quest for thermal comfort.

Present: We spend our time in a narrow temperature band, rarely venturing beyond our climate-controlled interiors. This sameness, regardless of place or season, dulls us to the fluctuations in nature.

Suggested Ideal: We should pursue passive temperature controls and shelter in our built environment to keep us safe but still connect us to tempered rises and falls as dictated by natural thermal gradients. In short we should dress and live more seasonally and spend much more time outdoors. If we spent more time outside — perhaps two to three times as much as we do now — we would become more resilient to and in tune with the elements and with the natural circadian cycle.

RATING: 8

TRANSPORT

Past: When we had no engines and or wheels, we were more connected to our local resources. Regional boundaries determined where we could travel and what we could bring home. People travelled on foot, and all of us were healthier for it.

Present: These days, the developed world is far too sedentary, relying on the automobile. Habitats have been designed to favor the automobile over the pedestrian, consuming too much energy.

Suggested Ideal: Returning to modes of transport powered primarily by human power would help us greatly. A secondary system using renewable sources would help us reconnect with life and nature as we move ourselves and our goods around our communities.

RATING: 8

HYGIENE AND WASTE

Past: Humans lived intimately with one another and other species. We had an extremely healthy microbiome and likely had hardy immune systems. Human waste was localized and, with low population densities and mobile populations, never concentrated. We actively participated in the nutrient cycle like all other species. Yet poor hygiene, illness and disease were often the death of us when we did not move away from our waste supplies.

Present: Antibacterial cleaning products and antibiotics have made us more vulnerable to germs by weakening our immune systems and destroying the beneficial communities we evolved with. Modern sanitation and sewage systems in the affluent communities of the developed world funnel trash and waste away, offering convenience and cleanliness at the expense of underprivileged neighborhoods and communities. Clearly, modern understanding of disease and pathogens has helped humanity immensely, even while many of our strategies to avoid them have been ill considered. Too often we send our "waste" away — resulting in health impacts to poor communities or other unintended consequences downstream.

Suggested Ideal: If we spent more time outside, we would re-engage with the soil — and all the bugs that reside in it — in a healthy way. People who spend more time growing up with animals are often shown to be healthier as adults. A modern understanding of hygiene coupled with an emerging understanding of the benefits of living in a healthy ecological community without over-sanitation would help people out immensely. Composting our waste rather than creating a larger problem by "shitting in water" would benefit us significantly, as well as the environment.

RATING: 8

INFORMATION, KNOWLEDGE & COMMUNICATION

Past: Oral traditions were once the only way to pass stories and wisdom from one generation to the next. Human knowledge was intensely local and deep. Technological and cultural innovation was slow, hard-won, and easily lost. It wasn't until key technological advances like writing that humanity's information and knowledge moved dramatically forward.

Present: Information is accessible to virtually anyone from virtually anywhere. Technology allows us to share and communicate with the world. This freedom of knowledge comes with advantages and disadvantages, but it is hard to argue with more knowledge as anything but good. What we seem to be lacking is wisdom, which is the productive application of knowledge. And we have also lost much of that knowledge that was intensely local and deep. We have, to our detriment, replaced knowledge of place and ecology with a broad veneer of trivial information.

Suggested Ideal: Humanity's quest for greater discovery and innovation is one of our better traits, and the democratization of good information that is now possible with modern technology is also significant progress. Yet much would be gained by remembering the wisdom of our elders, the wisdom of other species, and the important lessons from our long collective past.

> **RATING: 8**

HEALTH AND DISEASE

Past: Although our diet was more organic, our lack of understanding about human pathology made us virtually powerless against the effects of infection and disease. Healers relied on traditional medicine, magic, voodoo and sacrifice in an effort to cure. Without medicines to treat injury or illness, lifespans were shorter, but natural health remedies successfully dealt with some ailments.

Present: Modern medical technologies and innovations have enabled us to live longer (although many of the diseases requiring treatment are directly tied to our unhealthy ways of living) and enjoy a generally improved quality of life.

Suggested Ideal: We are very close to where we need to be in this category with constant medical advances, but our species could be measurably healthier if we took a more holistic view of health and treated the causes of poor health rather than just the symptoms. A society that focused on prevention and healthy living and treated all citizens with quality care would be considerably better, as would recognition of natural health paradigms when possible.

> **RATING: 9**

We have to temper our desire to control and tame nature, and choose instead to live in concert with it. We have to go back to seeing ourselves as an important part of the natural world, not separate from or superior to it.

As with anything, there is an ideal balance — a place where things are in harmony and optimal conditions are achieved; a sweet spot between the pre-industrial past and over-industrialized present; an internal "Boundary of Disconnect" that we cross at our peril. Of course, this theoretical boundary is never static. There has always been a dynamic interplay of forces. We are a durable and adaptable species, and many of our innovations have helped us immensely. But that doesn't discount the need for reflection and analysis.

There has to be a human-created environment where humanity is truly at its best and healthiest. Surely there is a set of conditions that best supports human wellness, culture, safety and life expectancy. Instead of spending so much money and time on technological and mechanized efficiencies, we need to focus resources on a much more critical analysis, one that examines the causes of many of the chronic problems that compromise human health, community and culture.

What would the ideal human environment look like? Let's consider the key elements of the pre-industrial past (pre-agricultural age),[7] the present affluent, developed world, and the ideal future. How far from ideal are we in each category?[8]

---

[7] It is important to point out that I am leaving out humanity's initial transition to cities and villages after the rise of agriculture, when living conditions for much of humanity became considerably worse before they improved. The average hunter/gatherer lived a healthier life than early city-dwellers.

[8] I'll be the first to admit that the scale shown is not scientific and is a generalized hypothesis — conditions would obviously vary greatly depending on location, era, climate, and year-to-year fluctuations.

Returning to all of the ways of the past is clearly not an option nor would it be desirable, but neither can we allow certain current conditions to remain unchanged. The direction we are headed towards even greater separation with the natural world is disconcerting. We have to temper our desire to control and tame nature, and choose instead to live in concert with it. We have to go back to seeing ourselves as an important part of the natural world, not separate from or superior to it. There are ways to apply our acquired knowledge that will benefit us, and our environment. We have to use technology as a tool — with discernment — to get our cities, our homes and our bodies back on the right track — to build communities that have a net positive impact on the world.

The habitat we crave is the one we need. We evolved in natural, biophilic settings, and it is incumbent upon us to recapture and preserve those same qualities within our modern habitat. Surrounding ourselves with life, spending considerable time outdoors and sharing our spaces with living things nurtures our kinship with nature.

Our love of life is what makes us human. So let's allow ourselves to get a little wilder and, where smart, to readjust our scales in the right direction. ■

Photo: Unsplash

JASON F. MCLENNAN

Considered one of the most influential individuals in the green building movement today and the recipient of the prestigious Buckminster Fuller Prize, Jason F. McLennan's work has made a pivotal impact on the shape and direction of green building in the United States and Canada and he is a much sought after designer, presenter and consultant on a wide variety of green building and sustainability topics around the world. McLennan serves as the CEO of McLennan Design and is the Founder and Chairman of the International Living Future Institute — a leading NGO that focuses on the transformation to a world that is socially just, culturally rich and ecologically restorative.

An Ashoka Fellow and an ENR Award of Excellence recipient, Jason is the founder and creator of the *Living Building Challenge,* widely considered the world's most progressive and stringent green building program. He is the author of six books; *The Philosophy of Sustainable Design, The Dumb Architect's Guide to Glazing Selection, The Ecological Engineer, Zugunruhe, Transformational Thought* and now *Transformational Thought II: More Radical Ideas to Remake the Built Environment.*

ABOUT

International Living Future Institute (ILFI)

The Institute is dedicated to leading a transformation to a civilization that is socially just, culturally rich, and ecologically restorative. It acts as a hub for visionary programs like the Living Building Challenge, Cascadia Green Building Council and Ecotone Publishing. The Institute moves across scales, offering global strategies for lasting sustainability, partnering with local communities to create grounded and relevant solutions and reaching out to individuals to unleash their imagination and innovation.

Ecotone Publishing

Founded by green building experts in 2004, Ecotone Publishing is dedicated to meeting the growing demand for authoritative and accessible books on sustainable design, materials selection and building techniques in North America and beyond. Located in the Cascadia region, Ecotone is well positioned to play an important part in the green design movement. Ecotone searches out and documents inspiring projects, visionary people and vital trends that are leading the design industry to transformational change toward a healthier planet.

Living Building Challenge (LBC)

The Living Building Challenge, the world's most rigorous green building performance standard, calls for the creation of building projects at all scales (from single-room renovations to whole neighborhoods) that operate as cleanly, beautifully and efficiently as nature's architecture. To achieve certification, a project must meet 20 rigorous Imperatives (including net-zero energy, waste and water) over a minimum of twelve months of continuous occupancy.

McLennan Design

McLennan Design is a regenerative architecture, planning, place-based design and product design practice focused on deep green sustainability, community and education that is dedicated to making significant and positive change in the world.

OTHER BOOKS BY JASON F. MCLENNAN

The Philosophy of Sustainable Design

In the Philosophy of Sustainable Design, McLennan outlines the major ideas and issues that have emerged in the growing movement of green architecture and sustainable design over the last thirty years. This book is intended as a starting point for anyone involved in the building industry on a journey to learn how they can build more responsibly.

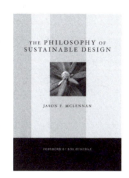

Foreword by Bob Berkebile

Zugunruhe: The Inner Migration to Profound Environmental Change

Just prior to periods of great migration, certain species display agitation and restlessness — a phenomenon referred to by scientists as zugunruhe. McLennan identifies a similar pattern emerging among people yearning for a sustainable future. This book is intended as a catalyst for anyone in-

terested in exploring a deeper, more meaningful connection to the environmental movement. Zugunruhe is a work of creative genius that draws us into an engaging journey of self-discovery, brings the biggest and most frightening issues of our time up close, and invites our engagement, notes David Korten, It will leave you envisioning human possibilities you never previously imagined. Profound, personal and practical, McLennan s narrative reminds us that individual efforts ripple outward and can lead to revolutionary change for the betterment of people and planet.

Foreword by Janine Benyus

Transformational Thought: Radical Ideas to Remake the Built Environment

Transformational Thought is a dynamic collection of provocative essays that critically challenge the design practices and thinking that are interwoven within our contemporary cultural, societal and personal value systems.

Foreword by David Korten